My Tiny Vegas

Life between the Sangre de Christo Mountains and the Great Plains

A collection of
real-life stories in and about
Las Vegas, New Mexico
by Birdie Jaworski

The author takes a hike outta town! / Photo by Berly Laycox

Mil Gracias

*This book was written for all of the residents of
my tiny Las Vegas, New Mexico.*

*Special thanks to Jane Lumsden who encouraged me
to collect my Vegas musings into this little book.*

The mighty piñon / Birdie Jaworski

Bienvenidos!

I live on the edge of the eastern plains of New Mexico, where the Sangre de Christo Mountains meet the Great Plains, smack in the middle of the town of Las Vegas. No - not the big "City of Sin" with the gambling strip!

Las Vegas, New Mexico is not as well known as other Wild West towns, such as Dodge City, Deadwood, or Tombstone, but she is said to have been the worst of the rowdiest Old West towns. She's still rowdy, still mysterious, still full of larger-than-life characters!

Doc Holliday kept his medical office in Las Vegas, New Mexico. The Rough Riders held their first reunion in the saloon of the Plaza Hotel in Las Vegas. You can get a shot of tequila in that same saloon, today.

I want to share my beautiful tiny Las Vegas with you...

Self-portrait at WarDancer Gallery

Traditions

Dime con quién andas y te diré quién eres.

Tell me with whom you walk and I will tell you who you are.

Huero Gonzales and Bruja / Birdie Jaworski

Trail of Chicos

Huero and Eva Gonzales stand among their chicos / Birdie Jaworski

The road to San Augustin passes nothing, nothing but a pistol-pitted sign welcoming travelers to county road C-24, nothing but dry wind and green-gold prairie, the asphalt twisting in deference to property line and gulch, pockets of fattened cows standing bored sentinel. I drove slower than the speed limit, my son riding shotgun, and watched the sun fall from my ears to shoulder in the rear view mirror.

A coyote stood at the edge of the road as if waiting to cross. Rough skin rose under her coat, a crisscross of scars and wayward tufts of fur. She looked like she knew something interesting about us, and I turned my head to keep her in vision. We watched each other until she became one with her fleas, a mere dot on the horizon, until my car edged past the Las Vegas Land Grant and into the Tecolote Land Grant at the edge of the Charles R Ranch. The late September sun framed her body, hung low in the sky, orange and swollen.

Louis counted two mobile homes, an ancient crumbled adobe, a simple stucco residence, another, until they disappeared behind us, until we turned with the road again and the plains turned to steep rock valley. I slowed to ten miles per hour, kept the car from sliding too fast down the canyon wall.

"Mom, we're almost there. Look, see the river?" I followed the line of his pointed finger across scarlet land to an oval protrusion of sage and rock and sunburned clay, the river nestled inside, and listened as he described the kind of thing only thirteen-year-olds notice.

"This is so New Mexico. It's a chile canyon."

I let the car coast as Louis rolled down his window, took deep breaths of rich valley air. "Yeah? Why is that?"

"The clay is red, and the plants are green. This is a Christmas canyon."

Louis was right. The land spoke of chile and reflected sun, all the shades of ochre and sage an artist can create, shades beyond any palette. Juniper and piñon broke the sun. The land spread in lumps among deeply irrigated soil, some places covered in mold-colored lichen, some places layered in gold and black dirt beneath a constant wave of tall grass.

A lone red-tailed hawk led the way, swooped high above the rocks then fell just inches from the road. His talons extended toward invisible prey. He was missing two flight feathers and the remaining ones were ragged and broken. The wind from his journey seemed to signal a temporal change. As we crossed the Rio Gallinas a herd of goats splayed from canyon wall to acequia. We left our world behind, our world of stock market bailout, of hungry consumer, of constant cell phone interruption. We traveled back in time.

San Augustin hides behind a swayed hogback ridge, a collection of adobe homes in various states of repair and a simple steepled church dating back centuries. The village looks tired, looks sleepy and forgotten, but looks are deceiving. A handful of men and women still work the land in the old ways, still follow the river of weather and moon in a pageant of goat, pumpkin, and chico. The land still breathes.

"I was born and raised in that house over there." Huero Gonzales sat in a pitched-roof adobe home, his back ramrod straight against a wooden kitchen chair. A ristra of ceramic red chiles dangled near his head as he pointed toward a simple whitewashed home across the dirt street. "I'm 74 already. I have eight children, twelve grandchildren, and six great-grandchildren now."

Huero motioned for us to follow as he walked through his house to the back door. A beautiful framed photograph of the San Augustin church taken in the 1970's graced the living room wall, paying homage to the community of faith that gave the village her name, gave her a refuge. Huero smiled as he told stories of the decades before his birth, stories of Apache raids against the village, when men and women of the village would gather at the sound of the big cowhide drum and teeter on top of the church's exposed vigas, ready to dump steaming hot water on the marauders.

"Now the church is only open one day a year, San Augustin's Day, the 28th of August," explained Huero's wife of 51 years, Eva Gonzales. "Huero built the sacristy of the church with his brother. Before that, people were going through the windows and stealing the saints."

Huero's back door opened to a yard resplendent with summer's final bounty. Rope strung from tree to porch to tree, every linear inch holding golden ears of roasted sweet corn whose kernels would become the northeastern New Mexican delicacy called "*chicos*." Some say the word chico comes from a Spanish word for something tiny. Others say it comes from the Pueblo people, comes from a similar-sounding Tewan word that means corn. Chicos have graced the tables of New Mexicans for centuries, sometimes slow-cooked in stews alone, sometimes with beans and pork and spicy chile.

Thousands of ears dried in Huero's backyard; thousands of hand-shucked ears first baked in a wood-stoked horno. The smell of fire and corn mixed with Huero's cigarette as he sat at a picnic table. The strings of chicos rustled in the wind, reflecting the afternoon sun.

"I only went through the eighth grade. I graduated from the IC School. I went one year over there." Huero bent low to pet his dog, Bruja. "I would walk on the weekends, walk all the way to McAllister Lake with the family goats and cows. It was my job to watch them. I used to saddle the horse, get the goats, while my mother made cheese."

The valley came alive as Huero spoke. I could see him chasing heifer and bull, collecting wood for fire, spending early mornings in prayerful walk past the church, courting a beautiful young village woman who would become his wife. Bruja seemed to grin, too, seemed to appreciate the stories of Huero's loyal working dog, a blue-heeler named Blue.

"I got me a job, four dollars a month cutting logs, not with a chain saw, a hand saw," reminisced Huero. "My hand would come out shaky. The next year I got a job catching the minnows in the river. I put some bread in the water, and I would scoop them into a crate. That was money in those days. I worked a team of mules."

Huero recounted the small jobs, the big jobs, the ways he kept his family fed during difficult times. He delivered mail to the villages of Trujillo and Maes. He began driving a school bus, taking children from the valley into town, a job that would remain his for thirty-five years.

"Everything is easy now," sighed Eva. "Those days, not easy. Everything is so easy now."

Huero jumped up to stoke the horno's fire. He added fresh pieces of dried wood. Flames licked the interior roof. Louis sat at the edge of the picnic table, his eyes riveted on the burning embers, his attention fully on Huero. The wind gusted, lifting the strings of chicos, shaking them like ghostly rattles. Huero pumped water into waiting buckets of fresh corn, then filled the horno with the soaked ears. He patted fresh clay made from his own earth around small cracks in the oven, sealing it shut with a broad, flat stone and more clay.

"The corn needs to sit in here overnight. In the morning, you can't believe how good it all smells. I make hornos for other people, and hope that more people in town call me to make them a horno. It's a dying art. Not many people can make them the right way, the way that will last." Huero squeezed his clay between his fingers, demonstrating the properties of his home-gathered earth. "If I make a horno in town, I have to haul the clay out there. This is the only place you can find clay like this."

The corn sizzled as the horno's flames leapt around the stalks. Smoke filled the backyard, the sweet smoke of harvest, of hard labor's pleasure, of traditions still strong and true.

"We used to wash the clothes, carry water from the well, we didn't have water inside or nothing. My mama, if we forgot something she would tell us you can't forget. You don't forget your rear end, because it is attached." Huero laughed, slapping his butt in a playful manner. "Life was so hard then. It's hard now, but I remember when it was much more difficult."

My son steadied a bag of chicos on his knees as our car wound up the canyon. Our clothes smelled like fall, like horno smoke, like Huero's words of cigarettes and memory. We lurched forward, in time, in space, until San Augustin disappeared behind us, her fertile valley awash in mystery, in the fading fire of Indian Summer.

The Green Machines

Green chile roasting in October / Birdie Jaworski

My lungs filled with the rich aroma of roasting green chile as I waited my turn at the gas pumps. Gabriel continued filling the tank of a tired elementary teacher. She slumped in the seat of her beat Ford Escort, head propped against the seat rest, as if five minutes of fuel could hopefully mimic twelve hours of good sleep. I realized she wasn't sleeping; her heavy eyelids meant rapture.

"Cómo estás, Birdie! You smell the chile? It's finally Fall." She reached outside her window and waved a plastic bag of cinnamon-laced biscochitos my way. I accepted a cookie, took a bite.

"Hey, thanks. I love chile season. I can't get enough of that beautiful smell."

The end of September in New Mexico means chile, means waxy green pods stuffed in burlap bags at the local grocer. New deep-red ristras can be seen hanging from balconies and porches, and men man caged machines where the green chile harvest is turned over shooting flames to produce a blistered skin.

Chile peppers have been a part of human diet in the Americas since at least 7500 BC, perhaps even earlier. Archaeological evidence at sites located in southwestern Ecuador show that chile had already been well domesticated more than 6000 years ago, thanks to its self-pollinating nature.

Chiles are considered a true superfood. Rich in vitamin C, a good source of most B vitamins - especially vitamin B6 - they also rank high in potassium, magnesium and iron. Health researchers believe that chile can help keep you cancer-free, can help reduce the amount of insulin required to lower your blood sugar after a meal, can help you shed unwanted pounds.

Chile is so important to New Mexico that it's been declared the state vegetable, even though scientists call it a fruit. Most historians credit Juan de Oñate, the Spaniard who founded Santa Fe in 1609, with bringing cultivated chiles into our area. He spread tiny dried chile seeds he carried from Chihuahua along his route, leaving them with native farmers, with mission monks, with the hope he would one day return to vibrant fields of fragrant spicy peppers.

The old monks roasted chile in the same manner we do today – over fire with a continuous flipping and tossing of the pods so that they are evenly blackened. You can see these roasters at various locations around town – at Lowe's, at Wal-Mart, in a backyard on 5th Street where a quiet man smiles at me as he turns his homemade wire machine. Sometimes I pause and watch him, watch his wiry arms load new green chile into the 55-gallon basket turned on its side, watch him close the hatch, rotate it over a fire fueled by canisters of propane. He concentrates on the chile as it spins, his brown eyes closed tight as if his meditation coaxes them to life, to the daily communion of red or green we take at each meal.

I watched a tall man in black jeans and a baseball cap spin green in front of Lowe's on Mill Street. He chatted with a customer as the broken black skin fell from the wire basket into a trough below the flames. Charles Brommer spoke to me as he fiddled carefully with the cage, made sure his customer's chile burned even and true. He shrugged his shoulders when I asked him how long he'd cooked chile.

"Just a month. It's my first season. It's a good job, a job where you know you're doing something important."

He laughed, as if roasting chile were actually a small thing, something un-important. His blue cap shaded his eyebrows, made him seem mysterious, a chile Ninja. But his dark eyes gave away his emotion, his connection to these long green pods.

"I love the smell. On a good day, you can smell it all the way up at Alltel."

I let my grin speak for me, let him know I loved his work, loved the way the sky rose with the scent of our ancient land. He smiled, too.

"I've lived here my entire life," Charles explained, "but I've never tired of this smell. I think I like green chile with enchiladas best. I also love it with eggs. I just don't like it too hot. Medium is best for me."

Charles cut open a burlap bag and hoisted the contents into one of two waiting cages. Lowe's customers walked past, most stopping for a moment to watch, to share a smile. Charles carefully adjusted a gas nozzle until hot flames covered the bottom of the machine.

"I let the machine do all the work," he mused. "There really isn't a trick. Basically I heat the chiles until the skins are burnt, then I turn off the heat and let them slow-cook."

Charles' customer waited patiently on a wooden bench while his chiles roasted. Joachim Romero pointed to the gray smoke as it wafted past us. He wore a dapper striped shirt tucked into pressed jeans, a man reverently dressed for the important yearly sacrament of collecting nature's finest.

"I've been living here for over twenty years, but my family was originally from Las Vegas here," Joachim said with emphasis. "My grandfather, José Leon Romero, helped drive the first cattle to this area and was one of three men who manned the Ilfeld store. I like chile real hot. I like it on everything. I eat it all three meals. There's no way I can eat any food at all without chile."

We waited as the chiles' skins puckered and sizzled, enjoying the aroma, enjoying the simple pleasure of sharing a sacred tradition. Charles brought the machine to a stop. The rotating basket shivered silent, its belly full, ripe with culinary promise. He emptied the chile into a waiting box lined with a heavy black plastic bag.

"I've roasted for folks from Colorado, Arizona, Texas - even a couple from Baltimore who never saw chile being roasted before," laughed Charles. He handled a scruffy broom and swept the small burnt skin peelings into a pile. "People use the roasted skins to feed their chickens. It helps clean them out and helps with laying eggs. I save these peels for anyone who comes and asks."

Joachim handed Charles a tip, then waved goodbye as he hauled his bag of blistered chile to his car. A fiesty crow hit the ground, gnarled feet extended, grabbed a smoldering piece of chile skin and charged toward the clouds. Birds don't carry the same sensitivity to capsaicin - the substance in chile that creates its heat - that humans do. Chile peppers are, in fact, a favorite food of many birds living in the peppers' natural range. In return, the birds distribute the promise of new life as the seeds are passed through their digestive systems unharmed.

Charles cleaned the roaster in preparation for his next customer. The crow circled above us, his body bathed in evaporating smoke. Charles ripped open a new bag and the scent of freshly picked chile mixed with the remnants of the last roast.

"On a good day I make twenty dollars in tips. Like I said, it's a good job. Ah," yawned Charles as he adjusted the height of the flames, "it just smells so good."

Pride in Piñon

Juanita Herrera (left) shows the author her piñon

If you can't pick who you want for President,
you can always pick piñon.

An old woman squats close to the ground next to a short, scrub pine. She wears a thick cabled sweater to protect her from the wind cascading across Starvation Peak. Her hands scurry through fallen needles, sifting for tiny elongated seed pods, dumping them by small handful into an antique five-gallon bucket made of tin.

"I shake the branches to collect the piñon," explains Mrs. Jane Yazzie, 83, of Bernal. "This is the way I learned from my Navajo grandmother. She learned how from her grandmother. Our family has picked piñon for centuries."

Mrs. Yazzie picks nearly fifty pounds of piñon each fall in the weeks leading up to Thanksgiving when the threat of icy roads keeps her tucked into her warm trailer home. She roasts her piñon the old-fashioned way, in an oiled cast-iron skillet stuffed inside a fiery horno.

"I grind the pinon after they cool off," Mrs. Yazzie says, her hands mimicking the motion of a pestle against mortar. "I grind them by hand, the way you should. It helps press out the natural oils in the nutmeat. This is how you make the very best biscochitos," she continued, referring to New Mexico's state cookie, "with a flour made from freshly ground piñon."

The piñon trees that dot our landscape live modest, long lives. They don't attain great height like California's giant sequoias. They don't shed a multicolored garment of jewel-toned leaves in the fall like New England's stately maples. Piñon - at first glance - appear to be lowly, humble, simple scrub conifers whose home between the desert and the high places speaks of solitude, whose gnarled limbs speak of nature's mercy. But the little trees have produced fuel, building materials, food, and medicines that enabled pre-historic Native Americans to establish their cultures on the Colorado Plateau and to survive into the present as the Hopi, Zuni, Pueblo, and Navajo.

"My grandmother told me stories about how our people on the reservation would pick piñon and store them in clay jars. They would dig pits in the ground and bury the jars to keep the piñon cool and safe. It's what got them through winter." Mrs. Yazzie breaks into a large smile and lifts a flecked brown pod to her mouth. She crunches into the shell, pulverizing both meat and protective coat. "I eat the whole thing. The shell has minerals and keeps you regular," she laughs.

Piñon seeds have sustained the people of New Mexico, Colorado, and Arizona for thousands of years, through rainless summers, through harsh snow-laden winters. The Northern Paiutes stored piñon in grass-lined pits, saving them for days when fresh grains and meat were scarce. The Navajo mashed the meat into a rich, oily spread like peanut butter to be eaten on hot corncakes. And local, Northeastern New Mexican tradition, holds stories of whole families and villages living on piñon alone during the dusty, drought-laden days of the dust bowl.

"I was a tiny girl, maybe five years old," reminisces Mrs. Yazzie. "I remember eating piñon for days. For weeks. It was all we had. We kept these big sacks filled with the last piñon harvest. My mother used to tell me that we were like piñon. We sometimes have a hard shell around us when times are difficult, but our insides are always sweet."

Mrs. Yazzie moves to another tree, this one at least a foot in diameter. She spreads a worn baby's receiving blanket under a promising bough and, standing as tall as she can on the tips of her toes, begins to shake. A cascade of nuts and needles rains onto the blanket, pelting the thin pink fabric with nature's Morse code, with the sound of hail across the grasslands, the flail of hooves against canyon floor.

"Nature makes the same sounds over and over," Mrs. Yazzie sighs. "To me, the sound of piñon hitting the ground is one of the sweetest sounds in the world."

She drops her arms to her sides eying the piñon's trunk. Short white hair stands out in tufts around her wide face. "You can tell the age of a piñon by the width of her belly. One foot across means that she is over 200 years old. Some of the piñon in this valley are nearly 1,000 years old. They have seen many, many things. I would not like to see everything these piñon have seen," she says, glancing at Starvation Peak, a thin, towering mesa where the Apache once tricked a group of Mexicans in 1837, leaving them to starve to death just out of reach of the piñon.

It takes three growing seasons to produce one piñon seed, twenty-six full months of work for the tree to sprout a new branch and grow the complicated prickly cones that house the seeds. Even though most people call them nuts, the protein-rich treats are the mature seeds of the piñon tree. Experienced pickers understand the cycle of good and bad seed years. 2008 has shaped up to be a bumper crop, with rich groves of piñon bursting with nutty promise across the forests of Northeastern New Mexico. Bumper crops rarely follow bumper crops according to scientists who study the species. The reasons why one year is great and another is slim are mysterious, and may have something to do with weather patterns as well as the tree's need for a solid carbohydrate base in order to create the cones.

Juanita and George Herrera of Las Vegas understand what it's like to follow the whim of the piñon tree. They sell seeds sealed in clear plastic baggies underneath a blue and orange Denver Broncos tent set up at the intersection of Mills and Grand Avenues.

"We pick at Rowe Mesa and at Mineral Hill," George, who works in the forensic department at the New Mexico Behavioral Health Institute, explains. "There's a ton of people picking this year. It's a good, solid crop this year."

The Herreras began selling piñon as a side business in 1998, and now have customers who drive from Raton, Tucumcari, and even out-of-state to buy their piñon in the fall. Rows of packaged piñon wait for hungry buyers, each labeled with a dollar amount written in black marker.

"I love being in the mountains," Juanita, a health worker who cares for the disabled, raves. "I just love it. It's my favorite part of picking piñon."

"I love being in the peace and quiet," adds George. "I love seeing and hearing the jets that fly overhead. That really tells you how quiet it is in the mountains, when one of those jets flies by."

Juanita and George pick piñon from morning 'til mid-afternoon on off-work days, from the beginning of the season in early October through November, until the first heavy snowfall cradles remaining pinecones in winter's blanket. Lifelong residents of Las Vegas, they both remember the traditions surrounding piñon from childhood, remember entire families carrying picnic hampers filled with good things to eat into the forest, running from tree to tree with child's pails, filling them with carefully collected seeds.

"It's still the same today," says George. "Families still pick together. It's an important piece of our life here. What's funny is how the technology hasn't changed. There's still no perfect way to pick piñon. You either have to shake the tree, pick by hand, use a dustpan and brush, or vacuum the branches. Nobody has a good method. You always get the piñon dirty," he continues, describing the bits of plant detritus and needles that come with the pods.

"We use a big screen to sift it," Juanita demonstrates, hauling a two-foot-by-two-foot handmade wooden frame with an inset mesh screen. "You pour the piñon in and shake to sort the nuts from the dirt."

George pours a bag of piñon into the shaker and points while Juanita uses both arms to shake the load. Needles and tiny bits of bark and dirt collect at the bottom of the tilted screen, while the larger nuts remain toward the top end.

"It builds big muscles," she laughs.

Juanita roasts her piñon in a microwave, the modern version of the horno. "It makes it easier to watch. They never burn this way," she says. "The stove takes too long and you risk burning it. But in the microwave, it always comes out perfect."

Piñon adds a delightful crunch to biscochitos and other cookies, to salads, cereal, granola, and provides a thick, oily base for pesto. One of the rare foods that can be used in most salty, sweet, and savory dishes, it is a well-rounded addition to every pantry. One serving of shelled piñon offers 14% of your daily fiber needs, 6% of your iron needs, and 6 grams of protein. In fact, piñon contains the most protein of any other seed or nut. To protect the nutritive value of the nuts, they should be kept in-the-shell in a cool, dark location. Shelled nuts should be stored in the freezer to keep the natural oils from going rancid.

A crowd of customers leans over the Herrera's piñon. A gust of wind crosses Mills Avenue, carries dust and bits of stray paper, but the seeds stay protected by the heavy canvas tent. A tall blonde woman from Texas selects two large pound bags of roasted seeds. She pats them lovingly as she reaches for her wallet.

"The best piñon comes from right here. I try to buy it every year from George and Juanita. I'm from New Mexico but live in Texas now, and you know what the two things I miss most are? Green chile and good roasted piñon."

Taming the Tree

My backyard in winter / Birdie Jaworski

The roads of Bernal skirt adobe home and coyote fence, roam past a cottage store where a curly-haired abuelita sells you cans of fizzy drinks and bags of spicy hot potato chips. She speaks with a soft voice, with the graceful lilt of her Castilian ancestors. She knows why you're here, why you let your car wheels embrace the frost-encrusted lanes.

Every road in Bernal is a back road, is a portal to another world, a landscape of written memory and lost time. If you let your eyes rest on the horizon, you can imagine the land as it breathed two hundred years ago. Wagon ruts rise to the surface, the scar of technology imprinted in red clay. The sun seems to cast shadow of Apache warrior and exhausted Calvary man against the wind-carved slope of Starvation Peak. The land sings a lullaby, a somehow sweet-melodied dirge that sifts through piñon and cholla.

These lands are more than merely ancient; they smell of the white sage that curanderas weave into smudge bundles; they smell of a rancher's finest horse, of blue merle cattle dogs and the sweat of fire-roasted chile.

And when the days shorten, when the bright New Mexican sun cuts a low swath across the sky, the roads of Bernal smell like Christmas.

The Santa Fe National Forest cuts through Bernal, stretches into the Pecos hinterlands. Every holiday season, beginning the day after Thanksgiving, local residents may purchase a ten-dollar Christmas Tree Permit, may pile child and dog and hacksaw into car, and travel the back roads into our timeworn forest and choose a symbol of the season.

Rachael Garcia sits in a rotating office chair at the Las Vegas Ranger Station on 7th Street. She wears a holiday turtleneck under a piñon green sweater. Her eyes sparkle as she gives the latest permit buyer the official rundown.

"You can go pretty much anywhere on our forest - Gallinas, Rowe Mesa, Bernal - it just depends on what species you want to find."

She glances at new permanent employee Vanessa Herrera with a hint of a grin.

"I want to test how well Vanessa knows her stuff. What kind of trees can people find out there?" Rachael tries not to flash too broad a smile as Vanessa pauses.

"If you're looking for piñon, then you want to go to Rowe Mesa," Vanessa replies, her voice measured, shy. "If you're looking for White Fir or Douglas Fir, then you want to visit the other areas." She smiles, knowing she passed the impromptu test, her wide eyes flashing in relief.

Rachael and Vanessa can issue your permit at the Las Vegas station Mondays through Fridays from 8 a.m. to 4:30 p.m. In addition to purchasing a permit, visitors to the station can select a Hermit's Peak T-shirt in a variety of fun colors and sizes.

"Be careful of the weather," Rachael warns tree seekers. "Make sure your vehicles are in order. We give each permit buyer a map of the area and a list of guidelines. If you are going out there, you need a good sense of direction and to be aware of the time of the day."

The official map shows shaded areas where cutting is allowed. Each permit allows the holder to choose one tree under ten feet tall. If you want a taller tree, you must purchase an additional permit. Commercial permits for vendors wanting to sell trees are available.

"As long as you're 30 feet from the road, you can take whatever tree you want," Vanessa adds.

"We also recommend that you pick your tree carefully and make sure it's the one that you want," Rachael cautions. "You can't cut one tree and then decide you really want another one. You have to tag your tree with the permit sticker before you cut. If you don't have the sticker on your tree and you are stopped, you will get into some trouble."

Last year, 100 Las Vegas area residents bought Christmas tree permits, and 500 residents from the greater forest district area - which includes Pecos and approaches Santa Fe - took advantage of the offer. A drive through the forest's roads reveals the occasional parked cars of tree-seekers, their footprints leading from road to trail in strange, circular loops, a beggar's walk from tree to tree, evidence of artistic examination.

"The Ranger Station guys usually pick good trees," Rachael praises. "But we've learned to work with the Charlie Brown trees in the office here. Sometimes we have one of those," she laughed. "I have had both piñon and fir. The fir trees are traditionally the most popular and look the most like the archetype Christmas tree, but the piñon smell so wonderful and are pretty, too."

Every year on December 7, I gather my family in my car and hit the I-25 frontage road, nose pointed toward Bernal, toward the mysterious twist of pine and history my ten dollar permit allows. It's my birthday treat, a tradition my parents first began when I was a young girl. This year I will turn 43, will let my children chase our dogs through the low brush, let them measure and contemplate each potential suitor. A tree is much like a lover, I tell them. We need to ask our tree for permission to take her home, ask her if she is willing to shed her life in the forest for a few weeks of party and lights. Some trees say yes. Some say no.

Last year, my older son Louis found his perfect tree - one I'm sure Rachael would have called a Charlie Brown special. Its trunk burped and dipped, its needles seemed to follow no master plan. He guarded it with his life as the rest of us shook our head No, tried to seduce another tree into giving up her ghost, another tree with a heavier shape, the golden mean of branch distribution. But Louis' tree is the tree that said Yes, please. As we tied her to the roof of our car, I swear she smiled.

This Sunday, look for me on the back roads of Bernal. I'll be the girl of 43, the girl with an orange permit sticker in her hand, the girl with a bag of hot chips and a can of fizzy drink, the girl with one eye on the strange land surrounding the trees, the other eye on her family.

La Salsa

Plaza Hotel details / Birdie Jaworski

My town held a Latin Dance Fiesta last weekend. The grocery store clerk stuffed the flier in my paper bag between a dozen free-range eggs and a package of dried pinto beans. Her braided silver bracelet caught the jagged edge of the bag and left a small tear.

"You gotta go. My boyfriend plays guitar with Son Como Son." She popped her gum with a pierced tongue and handed me two dollars and thirty cents change. Her hair hung in dry red-brown ringlets around a short neck. "You don't have to dance. You can just listen to the band and watch the Tango."

I hung the yellow flier on my fridge and stopped and read it every time I opened it for milk or jam or juice. Workshops in Tango, Cha Cha, Merengue, Cumbia, and Flamenco! The biggest dance festival in the county! Live Tejano music! All night dance party! I imagined wearing a dress spun like cotton candy and piling my hair high in a loose clip. I imagined dancing with a tall enigmatic stranger named Frito, a man with hair dark like licorice who would pull me too close, be dangerous with his arms and legs, lead my hips from the dance floor while his breath blew blue flames above my head.

I almost didn't attend. Babysitters aren't cheap and the workshops started at the rooster crack of dawn. But the flier taunted me, whispered dreams of dancing dark men from some crater moon, and I found myself shuttling my young boys to a neighbor's home while I zipped up the back of my sexy red dress with the asymmetrical hemline and buckled my vintage black dancing shoes. I took Avon, too, stuffed fragrance and bright red lipstick samples and two slightly wrinkled brochures in my small velvet purse.

I left my aging green convertible in the parking lot behind the dance party hotel. Two young women in ruffled Flamenco gowns smoked cigarettes, swapped a square compact back and forth. They leaned against a Camaro, wide hips splayed in provocative gestures, dark eyes painted with blue shadow and lined with more mascara than I use in a year. Tiny beaded roses dotted their hair, and I felt underdressed, old, missing the necessary traditional background of ground pork tamales and complicated saints. I stopped for a minute, pulled out my own small mirror and stared at the pinprick of red surrounding my left eye.

I've moved a mountain over the past few months. Feels like forever, like my life is starting over for the hundredth time. Who am I? Why am I doing this? I want to rest. I snapped it shut, even though my lips looked naked and the tip of my nose sparkled like wet glitter. I am ready for something new. I felt something fracture inside me. It thrust lightning bolts through my legs and burned through my feet, a trail of feathered fire. I stepped into the hotel.

The band caught my attention first, grabbed my ears and slung them like gunfire onto the dance floor, three middle-aged Mexican men with an accordion and two guitars, singing a song of loss and betrayal. The wood floor smelled of fresh honey wax, and heavy brocade curtains lined the windows overlooking the boulevard. Six couples faced the curtains, lifted feet and hands in almost unison and moved with the unpredictable wave of wind through an oak tree. My heart couldn't contain the rhythm of boots against floor. I wanted to join them, the band, be a worn guitar, a woman's stacked heel, wanted to melt into the pine boards beneath me in some strange captured surrender, but the sound turned to whisper and the dancers stood still, breathed one shot of air together, as the accordion player flexed his left hand, prepared to play.

"Excuse me, Miss? May I have this dance?" A tall Latino stood before me, the tip of his chin reaching the exact center of my forehead, and I remembered in desperation my collection of Avon samples. I wanted to say No, please sit with me and let's talk Men's Products, but the sadness in his eyes made my mouth say Yes, I will dance. He gently took my hand and led me to the center of the floor, the place usually reserved for the sure-footed and sane, and the strains of Felicia filled the hall.

"Thank you, Miss. My name is Manuel."

"I haven't danced in some years." Manuel apologized as a delivery truck idled outside the ballroom windows, setting the floor to rumble, the band to skip a beat, two, laugh, rest fingers, strings, voices. The dancers idled, too, moved legs in practice shuffle and arc.

"That's ok. I only know the basic tango steps. I will probably step on your shiny shoes." My eyes studied Manuel's cream-colored suit, the way it draped a body thick with muscle. I could feel his heart beat through his jacket, down his arm, into my right hand, chaotic, unsure. He wore dancer's boots and a bracelet made of an etched silver talisman strung on black leather.

He must be around my age, I thought. He has the same tired eyes, the same dark wisdom.

He smiled at me, his hair thick and wet with gel that smelled of amole and mineral oil. "Please don't worry. We can be useless together."

I liked the words he used, the way he hid something behind them, the quiet echo of his voice. The static truck faded to nothing. The band lifted instruments, and I heard the shuffle of couples moving into position. Manuel snaked his hand behind my back in a delicate wave as if he was afraid of breaking me into tiny pieces. He pulled me close and I heard him suck the air through my hair, breath the scent of my rosemary shampoo, my skin, deep into my skeleton, and I felt my body respond in the ways dance promises.

Allá en la casta apartada
donde cantan las espumas
el misterio de las brumas
y los secretos del mar,
yo miraba los caprichos
ondulantes de las olas
llorando mi pena a solas,
mi consuelo era el mirar.

The song told a story of an ocean of pain, and my feet slid right, then left, forgotten steps from some class six eons ago, but Manuel kept me steady, pure. I couldn't believe it, the way he danced, the way he made me dance. His frame covered mine, led mine, pulled me from a scratched pine floor to a dancehall in heaven, or hades, I didn't know which, only knew it undulated and fractured in a million pieces of motion and sound, captured my spirit and tossed it outside, made me grow a new one, a solid one full of blue faded slip twirl perfection. We danced beyond the center, into the outer rings of the hall, with dips and anchors no other couple attempted. I never danced like that, never let a man make demands of time and tempo, and I felt my heart match his heartache, match his syncopation, match his beads of sweat cascading from his forehead.

We danced six songs, watched couple after couple stop and stare, stop and rest, and we heard the band choose songs meant to snap us to eternity, until only our feet hit the boards, hit the walls, beat the band at telling a tale of madhouse redemption until I could dance no more. People snapped photos as we posed. I asked Manuel for a break.

"Let's sit and talk by the fireplace." I let my hand drop from his neck, pointed to a loveseat far from the music, and led him for the first time across the floor.

"Birdie, I have to leave. This is too much, too soon for me." Manuel stared at me through eyes dark and hesitant. "I just got out of prison."

I closed my eyes, my thoughts, tried to understand the fractal pattern of light and emotion we demonstrated in sidewinder grace for strangers who paid seven dollars for the privilege.

"Manuel, I don't care. Just sit with me and tell me your story. What is it? Drugs? Robbery? I don't care. You dance like an angel, like someone with the gift of physical prophecy. We can talk. We don't have to dance."

I wouldn't let go of his hand, tried to pull him to the couch, to a safe place to unload his misery, but his will was stronger, more focused, and he let me go in the middle of the ballroom as everyone watched.

"Birdie. I killed a woman I loved. Twenty-one years ago. I have paid my debt. Or I haven't. I'm not sure. I wanted to dance, but now I understand that I want the peace of it. I need to be away from women like you."

I watched Manuel run through the door. His body cast a shadow like Godzilla against the ballroom wall, and I willed him peace, willed him love and sanctuary. I wondered if he might have killed me if we continued, if our dance fell through eight levels of hell. The couples took their places once again, and I picked up my purse and slowly walked from the hall. I tripped in the place I last saw Manuel. My purse fell to the floor, fell open, and all my Avon samples spread in a pattern like our soles against the wood, like his sadness and my confusion, mirrored patterns of loss and redemption.

I left those samples strewn along the exit, left them to rot or use, walked into the pinprick of sun still left behind the row of piñon trees lining the street. The third-quarter moon stared at me, seemed to send me a message, something like laughter, something only the celestial can understand, something like love.

Cowboy Up!

Bean Day Rodeo / Birdie Jaworski

Around these New Mexican parts, Labor Day means the annual Bean Day Festival in Wagon Mound. Each yearly event features a free bean barbeque and the best rodeo this side of the Pecos! Of course I lassoed my two young boys and tossed them hogtied into the car with the promise of an American tradition. We didn't notice the band of black thunderclouds following us across the plains to Wagon Mound. We drank fruit punch from a community paper cup and passed around a plastic bag of kettle corn we bought at a farmer's market. My sons stared at the herds of antelope dotting the open range, at spires of chipped red rock rising from green pasture. A faded red falcon matched our speed, extended curved talons with a flat rise of his wings, grabbed something wiggling from the grassland.

We saw Wagon Mound from a distance. It sits on the old Santa Fe Trail, a mountain in the shape of a rumpled covered wagon resting in green dirt, overlooking the tiny Bean Day Festival. The sky grew heavy and dark as we drove through vacant old streets in search of the rodeo. We found it, a circle of cattle wire and pickup trucks on the outskirts of town. I pulled my Saturn into the entrance line, behind three farm trucks, all hauling livestock.

I diverted my boys' attention to a group of four straggly heelers. They ran along the fence, back and forth, each in line with the other, chasing cattle into a side pen. I paid a few dollars each for our admission and we made our way into the wooden stands. Maybe thirty other people sat in the bleachers with us, all rodeo folk, most waiting their turn in the games. A tiny girl in pigtails and jeans stared at my rhinestone-studded flip-flops. I wiggled one foot at her and winked. I rummaged through my purse and pulled out a few more dollars, gave them to the kids for the concession stand below us. They returned with nachos, burritos, a serving of Frito pie. We ate, watched the rains begin to fall as a parade of children and horses sauntered into the area. They carried two American flags and a bright yellow state flag.

Everyone stood for the Pledge of Allegiance. We continued to stand through the national anthem and then for an opening prayer in which Jesus was asked to spare any rider from harm. Funny thing was, when the prayers stopped, so did the rain, as if on cue, as if God herself waited to turn off the spigot. An announcer praised the breaking sun and the rodeo began!

I blushed those next few hours, time and time again. Not because I sat next to a handsome cowboy in mud-splashed jeans, but because the event held so much life. Cowboys hoisted themselves upon painted ponies. They held the horns of cattle, thighs squeezing cattle-back in mutual fear and ecstasy, tackling wild steer for the simple prize of a belt buckle.

A teenaged girl grabbed a rope and galloped into the ring. The mud sprayed across her chaps, her horse's mane, and she rose out of the saddle, leaned forward, tossed the noose! It hung in the air for a brief second, unsure where to land, then bee-lined for a crazy young bull, grabbing him by the horns. A lone cowdog howled "Hooray" from the sidelines, and the audience rose to applaud. She won first place, a silver buckle, and the men and boys cheered her as one of their own. I slapped palms with an old man missing two front teeth, his breath a symphony of green chile and tobacco.

The drive home was long and silent until Louis, 11, cleared his throat.

"Mom?"

"Yeah," I answered as my little Martin, 9, rested against the passenger window.

"People really are the same the whole world over, aren't they? It doesn't matter what they look like." He looked at the flying landscape as he spoke. An antelope ran alongside us, turned east, stopped short to watch us rumble goodbye.

"Yeah. We are all the same in all the ways that matter. I wish I were a cowboy."

I pictured myself leaping on a horse with a braided mane and a woven saddle.

"Me too, Mom. I wish that, too."

We watched the sun fall behind some unknown hill, the youngest son dreaming of Frito Pie and the few living things who can ride fast.

Sense of Place

El que nació para tamal, del cielo le caen las hojas.

The leaves fall from the sky for him who was born for the tamal.

Old Postcard

A Mom Called Paladin

A man walked across a desert wash. His black boots hit dry ground. His hand didn't hover near his holster. He let it match his stride, let it swing in a carefree arc that spoke of contentment, of a man fully present in his body. The sagebrush rustled, almost bowed in pleasure as he passed. I could smell it, the delicate oils the velvet leaves rubbed into his black pants. I could smell it, the purple sage, the gnarled piñon he leaned against as his steady eyes scanned the horizon. I could smell it though the sage swayed years before I was born. He knew the Bad Guy hid behind an outcropping of granite. He knew, yet his hand didn't meet the black strap of leather around his waist. The Bad Guy cocked his rifle. The man shook his head no. My son, Louis, age 12, flinched.

"Watch out!"

He yelled into the past, into the flicker of screen that channeled our consciousness, collected it, dumped it on the plains of San Augustin, 1960, 1860. He yelled at the man with the silver paladin on his hip, at the man who carried business cards etched with a challenge: *Have Gun Will Travel*.

He yelled, but the man didn't hear him. He didn't need to hear a young boy's warning, a boy who thought of himself as a man, a man with a black holster, a silver gun. The man moved like water, like the rush of spring rains down his desert wash, body and mind a symphony of sage and intellectual desire. The Bad Guy lay in the dust, clutching his arm.

I know my boy thought of this as we strode through the local flea market. I watched him move his hips like a hired gun through sage. It didn't help that *Have Gun Will Travel* looked like our rural New Mexico landscape; didn't help that our neighbors wore Stetsons, wore black boots coated in dry clay. Louis wore his black cowboy hat, his best dirty jeans. I wore mine, too. My youngest son, Martin, 10, raced to the end of the unpaved lot. The tail of his coonskin cap stuck straight out in the twenty-mile-per-hour winds. He sat next to a box of ducklings, fifty-cents apiece, and pulled out his wallet, open its frayed plastic cover. Empty. He looked at me. I shook my head no.

Louis stood at a card table covered in New Mexicana. A basket filled with dried red chile. A doll made of cornhusks and love sat on the corner. She watched over the table, one stitched eye larger than the other. She watched Louis pick up a black leather gun belt. I watched it, too, from the west, from my position twelve yards closer to the mountains, my position high and mighty, my feet closer to God. I saw him reach for his wallet, knew he had what it took, knew he never spent money unless he meant it. I shook my head *no*. He didn't see me.

Two decades ago I shook my head *no*. The Bad Guy didn't care. He tore my clothes from my body. He held a knife. He held a knife curved like an angel's wing. He held a knife to my throat. He tore my clothes. He raped me. One decade later I fought back. It wasn't too late; my mind could still escape. I bought a gun, a handgun forged of steel and hunger, bought a gun made for a man.

"We have smaller models. Perhaps something like this?"

The shopkeeper steered me toward a shelf sporting three tiny pistols. I stared at them, at the one with a pearlesque handle engraved with symmetrical curliques. I shook my head *no*. I bought the Glock, the heavy gun, the weapon that made me feel invincible, three-dimensional-sharp. I fired rounds at a plywood target painted with fear; shot it good, shot it plenty.

Shot it every sunny Saturday for two years until I killed that Bad Guy dead. I locked the gun in a case and slipped it under my bed.

The winds whipped through the flea market. The box of ducks tipped, and Martin ran this way and that, plucking one duckling into his chest, then another. I stood, frozen, the voice of God in my ear closest to the mountains. He whispered something, but I didn't catch it. The wind drowned His wish. Louis handed twenty dollars over the table. The corn doll flinched.

It's just a fancy tooled belt.

Thou shalt not kill.

My mind played tricks on me. My hat blew into the dust, blew twelve yards east until it landed at Louis' feet. He dropped his gun belt on the table, bent to grab my hat. He picked it up, brushed as much dirt as he could from the brim, then handed me both the hat and holster with both hands.

"Mom, I got this for you. You like Paladin so much, I thought you should look like him."

I turned toward the mountains, toward God, so Louis couldn't see my tears. I buckled the belt low and easy around my hips and plunked my hat down close to my ears. I turned, God turned, and the wind blew me into my boy's arms.

The next morning I slid the box from beneath my bed, the box that held my magic bullet, my returned life. I piled the boys into the car and we headed for the firing range. My gun belt pressed into the seat behind me. The winds slowed that morning, slowed to a crawl. I know God pushed them back, held them as I taught my boys the same lessons Paladin taught all of us:

Thou shalt not kill. But watch your back.

A Case of Mysterious Identity

My crazy house in Las Vegas, New Mexico

Vivian Vance and her sister owned the house I call my own. They lived in this simple cracked-stucco box on the edge of the Great Plains, where Mother Earth New Mexico gives birth to a flat-chested Oklahoman girl, a long-legged Texas boy. When Vivian as Ethel Mertz told Lucy Ricardo that she grew up in the Land of Enchantment, she wasn't kidding.

I imagine her tooling along the Turquoise Trail outside of Santa Fe in a silver-finned convertible while her handkerchief-covered curls catch white sage and sharp bits of tumbleweed. On purpose, of course. Vivian was that kind of gal.

Doc Holliday rented a room in what is now my backyard. Billy the Kid terrorized the locals; the Rough Riders held their first meeting eight blocks away; Kit Carson regularly rested across the street; the great Navajo Warrior Manuelito rode a gray horse along the Santa Fe Trail that still cuts my town into north and south. I could list the famous people who called Las Vegas, New Mexico home, a stopover, a place of commerce and good tequila, but it would take a ream of paper and more time than I've bought.

It doesn't matter. Vivian and her sister reign supreme.

Guero NightHorse laughs when I tell him this. He lifts his brown beaver felt hat and scratches his blonde hair. It's become Our Thing.

"Birdie, how can Vivian be more important than Manuelito? Even Kit Carson?"

I always give the same response, arms akimbo, my feet planted on the cement stairs of my front stoop.

"Guero, Vivian made people laugh. Besides, I can feel her presence sometimes. She and her sister. I think they visit this old place even though they didn't die here."

Until recently, Guero just nodded, wandered further down the street in search of something to do, something, anything other than lifting the bottle. He's not always successful. A couple of times a month he lurches past, doesn't see me, sees three of me, the scent of Tecate and fear rising from his lips. One of those days he stopped. I lifted my hands from my laptop.

"Hey, boy! What's up?"

Guero looked through me, as if Vivian Vance stood behind me, hands on my shoulders, reading my screen, the story that wouldn't gel.

"Were you serious about those spirits? Do you believe?"

I hesitated. Vivian lifted her palms from my shoulders. I felt her take one step back.

"Guero, I don't know for sure. I feel that we're more than our bodies. I've never seen Vivian, not really. But I can feel something here, some kind of funny presence. I did see my Grandpa's ghost once, when I was a child. So yeah, I guess I do believe."

Vivian smiled. I felt her grin raise goose pimples along my arms. A fat spider dropped from the porch eaves and twirled in front of my face - a warning, a roadblock. I shifted my body, let her attach a gossamer web to the iron railing.

"That's a Globe Spider."

Guero moved off the sidewalk onto my driveway. He approached my house, got closer than he ever had, repeated his words.

"That's a Globe Spider. They bring luck, Birdie. My people say they spin stories into their webs. Like in that book about the pig. Stories into their webs. You can't read 'em, but they can read you."

The spider didn't seem to notice his breath, the way it blanketed the porch with green chile and sour booze. I unconsciously lifted my hand to wave the smell west, but caught myself, let it drop. The spider continued to work. I pressed my glasses further up my nose and leaned close, too. One thread against the rail. Another from rail to step. Another from step to an empty ceramic planter that once held an Easter lily. Spin. Drop. Twist. Rest. She barricaded me from Guero, from the land, from the rest of the town I love, spun a story I couldn't read. I knew it was a story of isolation, of introspection.

This spider knows me too well. I'll have to remember to tell the boys to use the back door.

Guero straightened his back with a groan.

"Do you have any spare change? I know I never asked you, Birdie. I just need some money. Can't find any work around here since I got jailed for DWI."

I hesitated. The question frightened me more than ghosts. I knew my answer, though, the answer I always gave the homeless, the placeless, the ones like Guero heavy with psychic fatigue, with the certainty of unhappy death.

"Sure, Guero. Hold on."

I felt Vivian slip into the house as I opened the door. I reached inside my purse and grabbed what little money I had. A few dollars in change. I carefully held it around the web. Guero left without thanks, probably for the saloon, for another cheap can of beer, another slim dull moment. I slid my computer back onto my lap and stared at the forming web. I heard Vivian whisper into my ear.

We're all echos of history. You, me, Guero, Kit Carson, Manuelito, Doc Holliday, Billy the Kid. Only the spiders know us, know what presses us to ask for money, for more time, for another day of good health. Only the spiders know.

The spider lifted one leg as if to wave. Vivian floated above my head, floated above the cedar, above the catalpa. The spider chiseled another scene out of air and silk. A story of an uncertain woman, a dead funny lady, a man with unlikely blonde hair and a deep sorrow. A story only the innocent can read.

The Art of Death

Mount Calvary Cemetery / Birdie Jaworski

A young man I know fell off an outcropping of granite this summer, fell eight vertical feet, fell into a six-week land of cast and crutch and exotic metal pins. Shattered tibia. Surgery. June plans as broken, as painful as his swollen skin. I wanted to sign his cast, the blue sheath that hid the parallel scars, but he refused my pen.

"I don't want any signatures. I just want everyone to leave me alone."

I watched him hustle down my street, good leg out first, gimpy foot behind, dragging, dragging, rubber crutch-tip pressed into uneven brick, blue cast wrap coated with New Mexican clay, his armpits red with fury.

I told my dad about the man, the dirty cast, the way the sun refused to melt his disappointment. I couldn't read my dad's expression. He sat on a dusty shelf, in a five-pound box of unsifted crematorium dust.

"Dad."

I sighed, loud and low. My dog shifted her weight from one side to the next with a hollow thump. Her fur vibrated against the wood floor, echoed the song she expelled with one breath, another.

"Dad. C'mon. Gimme a sign. I just need one sign. One stupid sign. C'mon."

My dad didn't budge. His remains ignored me, ignored my exhaustion, my fingers stiff with forgotten words. He didn't need me, my pleas, my little-girl-lost frown. He sat on the edge of a galactic ocean, his body mingled with beach, with stardust, his mind so astral, so shattered, that any response he gave flew between the atoms of my heart, the quark and string that signaled it to continue, continue, beat, beat, continue.

The young man sat on his front porch, his bad leg extended, as my youngest son and I walked to the cemetery. The cast looked wary, heavy with dirt and anger. He didn't wave as Marty rose his hand in friendship, didn't move. I thought I heard a grunt, the shattered rale of ache against lung.

"It's too hot, Mom."

Marty lifted his baseball cap and wiped the sweat from his forehead. We'd walked two miles, almost three. The cemetery stood just out of reach.

"We're almost there, Honey. I've never seen it. C'mon. Have something to drink."

I held out a full bottle of water. My dad's ashes coughed. I felt it, three miles from my desk, felt him assemble and decay. Marty lurched forward, a robot on Mars, tiny robot with bio-skin near meltdown. He sipped.

The cemetery stole my heat, my fatigue. It rolled an acre, two, fifty, fifty acres of homegrown pain, of buried man, woman, and child. Marty chased a prairie dog, his robot battery satiated, aware. He didn't notice my surprise, didn't know the cemetery didn't look like a cemetery. I lost him to the pinon, to the prairie dog, the sky of stillness and fire. I didn't worry.

The plots didn't lie in elegant rows. They jockeyed for position, each facing the East, facing the rising morning Christ. Tiny iron windmills. Hand-carved river rock. Burned and etched slabs of pine. Dolls. Rosaries. Plastic

Marys with deliberately tilted heads. A handmade garden of death, only a few granite headstones in sea of a thousand, only a few memorials of Rich Person Passing.

I knelt to consider a baby's grave. The baby rustled beneath an uneven circle of hand-placed rocks. She danced with my dad, with my heart, with my boy chasing rodent, with the hardened heart of the blue cast owner. I couldn't stop the tears as a woman loomed into view. Pecos resident Lucia Martinez walked, a vase of dried sage in her left hand, from her cousin's home on Gonzales.

"I am an old woman now. Eighty-two years old, can you believe it? I buried my mother fifty years ago but the pain's still the same. I like to leave my mother something every few months. I can feel her watching over me. She was younger than me when she died." Martinez set the vase on a small cement kneeler. She looked past the simple wooden cross guarding her mother's grave toward the Sacred Heart of Jesus statue set into a sloping hill.

"I'm glad my mother is buried in Las Vegas. The city cemeteries have no heart. She died in Santa Fe, but the grounds there are too well-kept. This place still has real soul. She was born here. Look at the headstones. They're art."

Martinez pointed at a cross. It stood sentry over a thirty-year-old grave, simply etched with the decedent's name and date of passing along with a few gentle touches - a broad leaf, a decorative swirl. Behind her a working windmill chugged in time to the relentless wind. Beneath the twist of metal against air sat two new flower pots, each filled with living, watered mums, one on each side of a polished marble stone.

"Where do I want to go when I die? I haven't lived in Las Vegas for many years, not since I was a little girl. I want to be remembered here, though. I want my grandchildren to find my grave and leave rosaries and flowers. What use is a cemetery if no one cares to visit?"

Martinez turned to walk back to her cousin's house. She passed a pile of new teddy bears, one stitched with the word "Sister." She paused.

"See? This is what I mean. It's good to remember where we came from.

This place is real."

At yesterday morning's flea market I added a smiley face in Sharpie black to the exposed skin of a scarred leg. The young man's frown shattered. He smiled, the first time in six weeks I saw teeth, saw his open future. My dog smiled too, her haunches spread against dry clay, in her vibrating fur blanket. My dad didn't smile, but the dead don't grin.

Cloud Dancers

Aztec Dancers at the Fiestas / Birdie Jaworski

My town drinks from a river that forgot how to run, under a sky that forgot how to cry. Most townspeople call it the "Mighty" Gallinas, though a week ago it ran nearly dry, barely trickled past sun-punished reeds. You could drop a match and light the sky. You could breathe the local green chile stew and ignite the trees, evaporate the train station, the haunted Castaneda Hotel, the dilapidated roundhouse. The city administration voted extreme drought rules into effect a few months ago. No watering lawns! Restaurants can't wash coffee mugs, and the other night I walked past the restored Wild West hotel where Roosevelt's Rough Riders held their first reunion in 1899, stood at the window, watched the bar where Doc Holliday held medical court. The bartender mixed good gold tequila and fresh lime in a salt-rimmed Dixie cup. Tough times.

My skin caught dust like my car windshield, left a soft patina of grime along my bare legs, my arms. Most days I kick my cowboy boots against the ground, let the loose dirt fly to heaven. No grass keeps it close to the ground, nothing alive, nothing awake beneath my feet. *Please rain*, I asked the blue above me, asked God, asked anyone, anything who might listen.

Please rain. Please help us. The Gallinas continued to fade.

My neighbor shrugged his shoulders when I brought up the endless sun.

"Birdie, this is nature's circle. We must complete the cycle. Rain will come when it's time."

I remembered his words when the hint of monsoon began in the days before Fiestas, when sparse rains left the suggestion of water against the parched earth. A few sprinkles here, a handful of hail there, maybe an inch in a week. Not nearly enough to swell the river and give us hope.

I walked to the Plaza to enjoy the party music, plenty of sunscreen slathered on my bare arms. I could hear the primal beat of a taut drum. Five dancers shook the dance stage, three women and two men in feathers and beaded leather, the Danza Azteca de Anahuac. Tiny walnuts tied to their shoes made the noise of a rattlesnake as their legs and arms moved in unison. The scent of piñon incense rose above them, rose in prayer. The men pounded flat, octagonal drums while the women shook rattles made of turtle shell. They paused, bent low to the ground in thanks, then faced the audience.

"We just came from Monument Valley where we danced for rain. Now we'll dance here in Las Vegas for rain. Please join us on the stage if you'd like to dance for rain, too."

I hesitated, but only for a moment. A small stream of people filed onto the platform, moved between the Aztec dancers. I climbed the stairs and found an empty spot near a dancer with sparkly embroidered snakes on her ornamental gown. The dance began, and I followed the motions of the music shamans who traveled such long distances to bring water from the skies. I lifted my legs, my arms, my eyes in time to the drums. The sacred smoke burned my throat but I didn't stop until the last vibration of mallet against skin blew with the wind to the Great Plains.

I walked home, the sky still bright, still casting sour shadow on the ground.

The rain dance didn't work, I thought.

An hour later the skies grew sleepy, grew dark. The rains fell, fell hard and restless against the ground.

Ladybug Migration

Hermit's Peak / Birdie Jaworski

Hermit's Peak looks alien, looks sharp against our softly curved sky. The mountain is littered with crevices and caves, its peak rising 3700 feet above Las Vegas. The monolith was once called *El Cerro del Tecolote*, The Hill of the Owl, by early Spanish settlers. Old stories tell of a wise feathered messenger from heaven who reminded travelers to watch, to listen, to stop and pray.

"God's owl used to protect those who had to face the mountain," explains Mona Gallegos, a tiny woman from Mora who used to serve lunch in the schools. "My abuelita told me to stop when I heard the owl. That meant it was time to notice God's beauty and ask Jesus to help me get through the day. Now I tell my own grandchildren to listen for the owl when they make their pilgrimage up Hermit's Peak."

In the late 1800's, the mountain took her new name. An Italian missionary, Juan Maria de Agostini, called a natural cave near the tip of the summit home. He came to be known as a holy man, a man whose hands held God's healing powers, a man who traded carvings and trinkets for food.

Each Good Friday, pilgrims the Spanish call *Penitentes* carried lighted torches up the steep trail, praying for forgiveness. Hand-hewn crosses still stand near the overlook, each surrounded by new devotional candles and rosary beads, and the hermit's source of water, an underground spring, waits for tired hikers to drink from its cool, clean depths.

People aren't the only ones making journeys up the mountain, aren't the only creatures following an unspoken call. The hiking trail up the mountain's rugged folds is difficult, beset with what feels like thousands of switchbacks. Her summit lays flat, a broad park-like area with imposing cliffs on the eastern and southern sides. And in the fall, when the golden aspen catches September's sun, the ladybugs return.

The ladybugs arrive from aphid-infested wheat fields in Texas and Oklahoma, fat, happy, engorged on farmers' pests. They congregate in the high-lying areas of Northeastern New Mexico, in the places far above the Great Plains. They visit during Indian summer, roll in the deep cracks of broad-leaved agave, the spines of pale green western grass. They hibernate here, find warm holes in the ground, dark corners where they can rest and wait.

Hikers will find September's peak covered in millions of Convergent Ladybug Beetles, *Hippodamia convergens*. They sneak into every fold of leaf, every cactus crevice, clustering close to protect each other from fall's growing winds. The beetles get their name from the converging white lines on their thorax. They usually have 13 black dots on an orange elytra or shell.

Each summer at Hermit's Peak, a new generation of ladybugs participates in a passive, or wind-carried, migration. After feeding all summer, they hibernate through the winter, their bodies cold, lifeless, underground. Ladybugs don't navigate well. They can fly short distances, jump from one branch to another. They need our spring winds to carry them home. They may land in the arid plains surrounding Roy and Mosquero, or, if luck is a ladybug, they will find Texas' bounty.

During a lifespan of a few months, female ladybugs lay up to 500 eggs on leaves and twigs. The eggs hatch and the larvae engorge themselves on aphids, then pupate. Since the larvae clean out the fields, the adults migrate back to Hermit's Peak to await the opportunity when they too can go back to aphid-rich areas and lay their eggs.

Last fall brought an abundance of ladybugs to the hermit's haunt. On a sun-drenched Saturday, I pressed aching feet into the steep grade, my right hand moving in triad instinct as I passed each Station of the Cross. I didn't see ladybugs until I lifted leg onto the summit, until I glanced down at my feet to see them surrounded by a gentle army of delicate orange beauties.

The beetles didn't notice me, didn't fly in fear. They continued gorging, their bodies soaking sun as they splayed across any available succulent. And in the distance, beneath the sheer drop of stone cliff, a lone owl welcomed me, reminded me to stand in thanks, in wonder, to ask for help on my way down the mountain.

New Home on the Range

Wind River Ranch's Bison / Birdie Jaworski

Three hundred years ago, the storm and thunder of bison swarmed the piñon-laced hills outside of Las Vegas, New Mexico. The land looked different then. Beaver claimed the Rio Gallinas in numbers much larger than today. The river bent to nature's whims, snaking around geological dips in the landscape, flooding the plains during spring thaw.

The land grew wetter, greener, more dense. Prairie dogs dotted the landscape with cavernous burrows, their chewing of native grasses prompting the tender shoots that bison love to explode across the plains.

It's difficult to imagine how Las Vegas and our surrounding communities used to appear before cattle barons carved the land grants and shifted the balance of natural power, forced thick fence stakes into the red earth in order to keep the neighbors and bison at bay, before fur trappers scented rusting traps with the glands of dead beaver in the hopes of snagging a fat prize.

Dr. Brian Miller, lead biologist at Wind River Ranch, a 5,000 acre ranch near Watrous devoted to ecological restoration, research, and education, understands that the delicate balance of nature has been upset, but can be restored. The ranch is currently owned by the EC Thaw Charitable Trust and is leading a cutting-edge research program of reintroducing keystone species such as bison, prairie dog, and beaver, in addition to rebuilding critical wetlands, with the hope that the native landscape will slowly recover. Dr. Miller, who is widely known for his decade-long work with the conservation of the endangered black-footed ferret, served seven years as a Coordinator of Conservation and Research at the Denver Zoological Foundation.

"We began grazing bison in June 2007 as a result of talks with several tribes about sharing a herd," explains Dr. Miller. "With enough partners, that herd could be moved from place to place to more closely mimic the historic movements of bison. The Cultural Affairs Office of the Jicarilla Apache wanted to start a herd of bison on their tribal lands, and we are trying to give them a head start by grazing the bison on the Wind River Ranch. We view bison as a significant commitment to restoring grassland health and native species diversity. Indeed, of all the wild ungulates that were nearly pushed to extinction in the late 1800s, only bison have not recovered in the wild."

43 bison now consider Wind River Ranch home, most of them new acquisitions from the Cultural Affairs Office of the Jicarilla Apache Tribe. The bison have been relocated as part of the efforts of the InterTribal Bison Cooperative (ITBC), a group which coordinates and assists tribes in returning the buffalo to Indian country. In prehistoric times, millions of the thick-hided muscular animals roamed the continent. No one knows how many bison there were, but the naturalist Ernest Thompson Seton estimated their numbers at sixty million when Columbus landed. They were part of the largest community of wild animals the world has ever known. By the late 1800's, only three hundred specimens remained, and today's slowly blooming populations are direct descendants of that small herd.

"Bison are an integral part of the prairie grassland," Dr, Miller says. "The present grassland was formed largely due to the activities of prairie dogs and bison, two highly interactive species. In their absence, grassland health declined, despite the introduction of another large grazer, domestic cattle."

Wind River's new bison travel across the grass-laden lands as a herd. They appear to move as one unit, sharing one mind. When a threat - a human, a vehicle - appears, the herd moves together, rising, running, muscular flanks pounding into the crusty earth where indigenous grasses once grew. They face heavy winds as they rest, thick bodies pressed into dry ground, heads erect, steady, giving the bison an air of self-reliance, pride. The new herd members quickly acclimate to the ranch's older group, learning the pecking order, the places where the sweetest grasses grow.

Picuris Pueblo member and ITBC Secretary, Danny Sam, recalls how the reintroduction efforts began with only a bison bull and a cow. He stands with hands in jean pockets, a baseball cap protecting his head from the ferocious wind, his back to the bison corral, a black metal enclosure where the new bison rest until a veterinarian checks their health.

"We started the herd as a sustainable food source for our tribe. A lot of indigenous food has been taken out of our diet," Sam explains. "The Inter-Tribal Bison Cooperative consists of 57 tribes in 19 states. Nine of those tribes are in New Mexico - the Taos, Jicarilla, Apache, Cochiti, Sandia, San Juan, Picuris, and Tesuque tribes. We trade bulls to keep the gene pool diversified, and we market the meat at the Santa Fe market as well as other locations. It's a lean meat, very healthy. We keep the bison wild. We don't want to 'cattle-ize' them. Let buffaloes be buffaloes."

The ITBC hopes to provide free or low-cost bison meat to tribal members, especially those who suffer from diabetes and other health issues for whom the lean un-marbled meat is highly recommended. The cows have a nine and a half month gestation period, producing one offspring per year. The calves - born with red fur - jump to their feet within ten minutes of birth, where they blend in with the local clay.

"All of the bison cows come over and lick the calf," explains Sam. "Each one has a personality, a name. One of the calves we named 'Holly' because she was born near Christmas. People don't realize that they run faster than a horse. They are less pressure on the ground, too, and spread seed through their woolly coat and dung."

The wind picks up some afternoons, scattering dust along a deep river canyon dividing the ranch. The bison don't follow the tick of clock, the whims of any curious visitor. They hide deep in scrub pine where shadow meets shadow. Prairie dogs furiously dig burrows, aerating the soil which sustains the bison's grasses.

Danny Sam laughed as a frisky cow pushed another against the corral.

"A whole ecosystem existed that was based on bison along with prairie dogs and natural predators like the wolf. Finally, men are beginning to realize the value of bison and other keystone species once more." Sam paused to watch the cows challenge each other. "We're grateful to Dr. Miller and Wind River Ranch for allowing us to preserve our heritage and help our mother earth flourish once again."

History

El diablo sabe más por viejo que por diablo.

The devil knows more due to being old than by being the devil.

Calumet Says Howdy mural / Birdie Jaworski

Ghost Plane

Lindbergh lands in Las Vegas, New Mexico

80 years ago this month, a young man sat on the edge of dusty forever. His airplane's wheels dug into dry prairie. He didn't know the grass would soon lift from the earth and rage across the Great Plains in the clouds of fury and death that marked the Dust Bowl.

You can see this man against an interior wall in the Las Vegas Railway Depot, his handsome face covered in aviator's goggles, encased in framed glass. Two men stand behind the fuselage. They hug one another, dark intertwined shadows against the drought-scarred land.

The Las Vegas Chamber of Commerce leased the parcel beneath this plane one year before, plunked down earnest money for a 40-acre pasture. They drove out herds of thin cattle, a small handful of poor squatters, and declared the parched earth an airfield. A local booster club gathered their men, carried buckets of thick white paint and heavy boar's-hair brushes to the pasture. They followed Herbert Hoover's strict orders to label their space, painted "Las Vegas" on the hills, a careful circle around the airfield, on the evaporated land so that future aircraft would know they would be welcomed with home-cooked meals, a stuffed cotton bed. The paint dried quickly in the New Mexican sun. The men looked at their creation and added an arrow so that wayward pilots could find the landing strip, even though one was not yet smoothed into the crusty surface.

The residents of Las Vegas patted each other on the back. Not many cities in the Southwest sported an official runway, a place of potential international commerce. Men visited the spot, sometimes taking wives bearing reed-woven picnic baskets filled with green chile stew and tortillas. No planes touched down, not then, not yet, but the city people knew it would soon happen. They added gates at both ends of the field for fuel trucks, and a tall windsock made of tight white canvas.

The budding airfield caught the eye of Transcontinental Air Transport. TAT sent a courier to northeast New Mexico with an important letter. *Las Vegas may be one of our official stops*, the letter read. *Your town may be famous, a place where weary travelers stop on coast-to-coast journeys. We're sending our president*, the letter continued. *Expect a visit from Charles Lindbergh on October 23rd*.

Thousands of Las Vegans packed the airfield. Children carried tiny American flags sewn onto rigid sticks. Women wore their Sunday best and gently pressed fancy combs of glazed horn into their hair. The sun shot patterns of long-legged men across the soil as the people held handkerchiefs to their noses. A deafening cheer broke the wind's howl when Lindbergh landed in a black plume of exhaust.

This moment echoes forever in the Depot's waiting room. The hugging men speak for Las Vegas, for a future not yet realized, not yet understood, a future desperately wanted. The TAT didn't share that hug. They chose Clovis as their official stop. Las Vegas kept right on leaning into the prairie wind. The City caught Lindbergh's passion for flight, and eleven years later - after depression, after a decade of sifting dust - opened the airfield to regular traffic.

The first major construction at the Las Vegas Municipal Airport began on April 1, 1941 under the supervision of the Army Corps of Engineers, and in the summer of 1942, city officials opened the field with a solemn celebration intended to echo the gravitas of war. The first airport facilities included a communications station, a rotating beacon, a small brick building for Continental Air Lines, and a hangar for New Mexico Highlands University.

During World War II, the Navy used our airfield for pilot training. New Mexico Highlands University sent students to its hangar - then a classroom and workshop - training aircraft mechanics for defense work. After the war, the aircraft mechanics program branched out, with the university offering a two-year airport operators' course until government support for the program ended after the Korean War. Today the Las Vegas Municipal Airport consists of two asphalt paved runways, with an average of 13 airplanes served per day during summer's warm vacations and six per day in the depths of winter.

Lindbergh never visited Las Vegas again. But somehow he still lives here, on the edge of the grasslands, just behind the train tracks, on a quiet wall only travelers see. His face is hidden in shadowbox glare, and his adventurous spirit radiates, flies past the perceptual boundaries of time and space, lands in the hearts of all Las Vegas' people.

Footsteps of Time

Dino tracks at Clayton Lake State Park / Birdie Jaworski

Twelve miles north of a sleepy Northeastern New Mexican town, the invisible ghosts of majestic beasts roam the outskirts of a manmade lake. 100 million years ago, claw-toed and sloe-eye monsters jockeyed for position here, fought for tender greens, for succulent flesh. The guttural cry of flying reptiles - wingspans as large as 40 feet across - echoed against an ancient seabed. Driving through the burg of Clayton, you may think you travel through an area worn and heavy, an area still smarting from the ravages of the dust bowl, from the decades later when newly-paved Interstates stole drivers, asked them to forget the quirk and charm of small-town America. But the land holds deep secrets, holds the memory of lush tropics where dinosaurs once lived, and at Clayton Lake State Park, holds over 500 viewable Early Cretaceous footprints.

"I lived here my whole life and never did go see them tracks," muttered Clayton resident Joseph Warner. He stood with his back to Shrine of the Testaments, an art gallery featuring biblical history, primarily the oil paintings of the late Jan Maters, a Dutch-born, classically-trained artist. "I do believe humans and dinosaurs existed at the same time five thousand years ago. I believe in the bible."

Most scientists tell another story, however, one of a shallow oceanic strait that connected the Gulf of Mexico with the Arctic Ocean. Called the Dakota Group, the rocks formed along the Western shore of this seaway are rich in the most ghostly remnants of the dinosaurs - their tracks. These footsteps are made even more eerie by the fact that no dinosaur bones have been found in this part of the Dakota Group. The shallow imprints carry the only evidence that dinosaurs lived at all in this region.

The most common tracks at Clayton Lake, and indeed throughout the "Dinosaur Freeway", are broad, three-toed tracks. The largest of these tracks is about thirty centimeters in length, from the tip of the middle toe to the rear. Similar tracks have been found in Brazil and in England. The tracks were made by ornithopod dinosaurs, large herbivores. Ornithopod means "bird-feet," and as one stares at their fossilized footprints, one can't help but laugh at the thought of huge thick-skinned beasts running on what might have looked like chicken legs.

In the rolling grasslands of the extreme Northeastern corner of New Mexico, near the carve of wheel rut into hill that marks the Santa Fe Trail, an earthen dam was constructed in the 1950s across Seneca Creek that resulted in the formation of Clayton Lake. The excavation of the spillway, and a flood in 1982 that swept away a thick layer of silt from the spillway, uncovered an unexpected bonanza of dinosaur tracks. Researchers from every corner of the globe raced to the tiny town of Clayton to study the fantastic find.

Today, the tracksite, with over five hundred dinosaur footprints, is one of the world's best-preserved and most extensive. A sheltered gazebo and boardwalk were built along the trackway, with comprehensive information about the kinds of dinosaurs who lived here so long ago. At least eight different varieties of dinosaurs left their marks on this ancient mudflat, evidence any visitor to the State Park can see.

The best time to see the tracks is in the two hours before sunset when the sun casts low shadows against the white-rocked spillway, giving them added dimension and contrast. The park is often silent, empty, its simple wooden boardwalk belying the significance of its famous footprints. As one walks around the tracksite, one sees a cornucopia of definitive tracks, unambiguous monuments of the incredible creatures that once owned the land.

"I can't believe no one is here," mused young mother and Raton resident, Theresa Lovato as her first-grade son ran ahead on the boardwalk, eager to see the dinosaur tracks. "It took us a few hours to get here, but this is worth it. I can't believe no one else is here," she echoed. "This is one of New Mexico's finest gems. I remember seeing the tracks a few years back in high school. We took a fieldtrip out here and our teacher pointed out a place where you could see not only the footprints but a track made by a dinosaur tail."

Lovato's son stopped cold as he spied his first set of prints, a series of five deep three-toed depressions facing the lake. He squatted low to the wood walkway and leaned his buzz-cut head over the tracksite in order to get a better look.

"Look! Look! Dino tracks!" He yelled, but kept his eyes on the rock-hard mud.

Clayton Lake contains examples of parallel trackways, areas where the dinosaurs may have ventured north together. At Mosquero Creek, an arroyo-surrounded site south of Clayton Lake, at least 55 trackways of small ornithopods have been found, all parallel and all trending towards the north. The "Dinosaur Freeway" may have been just that - a migration route spanning north and south over hundreds of miles of forgotten shore. Visitors share in the ancient energy, imagine the ghostly cold-blooded creatures as they let the sun set over the spillway.

"Dinosaurs. Dinosaurs. I don't know what God had in mind when he created those dinosaurs," laughed Joseph Warner. He flicked the ashes from his cigarette into the street. "I think if they were alive today, we'd keep them in a zoo. They wouldn't have their freedom. Maybe it's better they died off a long time ago."

Sanctuario de Singularity

Chimayó / Birdie Jaworski

Both my sons stared at me Saturday morning. I sat on my bed, surrounded by piles of product, padded envelopes, my heart determined to catch up with work. My arms couldn't meet my desire, shook from fatigue as I carefully inspected each item.

"C'mon, Mom. Let's go do something. We haven't gone anywhere in weeks." My oldest son, Louis, 11, accented weeks as though he were a prisoner in solitary confinement fed on moldy bread and stale water.

"Yeah, Mom." Martin, 9, picked his nose as he agreed with his older brother. I leaned over, grabbed him a tissue from the night-stand.

"All right. We'll go on an adventure. But I get to pick the destination!"

The boys helped me fill sport bottles with the mineral-laden town water. I threw cheese puffs and trail mix in a large zip-lock bag and added a hand-ful of chocolate chips and a generous portion of chopped walnuts. I stood, bare feet on kitchen linoleum, and decided what wilderness we would visit. Someplace quiet. Somewhere gentle. The village of Chimayó. I almost left the house without Avon, but tossed ten samples of the new Avon Super Shape Anti-Cellulite Stretch Mark Cream in my purse.

Two hundred years ago, a Chimayó friar was performing penances when a brilliant light burst from the hillside. He dug into the ground where the light appeared. His hands found a crucifix. The head priest brought the crucifix to a fancy church far away, brought it to be venerated, but three times it disappeared and was later found back in its hole. Then the miraculous healings began, healings associated with the dirt surrounding the artifact.

I told the boys this story as we drove through the parched mountains west of my town, told them about the Chimayó chapel, and the way the newly-whole left crutches and before-and-after photographs in thanksgiving.

"Geeze, Mom. You believe that stuff?"

Louis spoke with a mouth full of snacks in the backseat. He cocked his head to the left, the way he always does before he explodes in a torrent of intellectual excess.

"According to historical research, there is no evidence that Jesus was divine. In fact, one could make a case that he never existed at all."

Louis continued, his words some kind of middle-school version of the DaVinci Code. Martin didn't pay attention. He leaned against the car door, a clipboard balanced on his knees, as he drew illustrations of penguins in space.

I didn't answer. I kept my hands on the wheel, let my car slide past one herd of antelope, then another. They raced the wind, thirty, forty, fifty moving as one beast, a mass of delicate antler, of striped flank, of hoof-earth unison. Even though it was Memorial Weekend, we didn't pass another car.

Chimayó snuck up on us. We fell from the mountains into the desert, with short sun-faded scrub and piles of white sand, fell into a village of a few adobe houses, a shack selling last fall's piñon and cheap religious trinkets, and the old chapel of miracles. A small dirt parking lot sat in front of the chapel with enough room for perhaps three dozen cars. *Handicapped Parking Only*. The blue sign spoke of hope, of the people who pilgrimage to Chimayó. We parked half-a-mile away, under the sparse shade of a mature cottonwood.

The church welcomed us with a sheaf of red desert roses overhanging the open wooden door. We filed inside, behind an old Latina in a wheelchair and her young caregiver. The chapel looked like nothing and everything at once. The walls were cracked brown adobe, tired, carrying the energy of a million broken people. Low wooden benches rested in uneven rows. Twenty or so visitors knelt on hard pine kneelers, their hands clasped in prayer, their eyes on the painted altar. Mexican saints surrounded us, their peeling fingertips pointing toward Heaven. The boys watched the flicker of a thousand votive candles. I pointed to the famous crucifix, to the hundreds of rags and crutches and photographs piled along the church sides.

Louis found the holy dirt site first. A depression sunk into the church floor, a child's orange plastic shovel helpfully left inside. He bent low, dug into the ground, handed me a shovelful of healing dust. I found a tissue in my purse, opened it, let the dirt collect inside, folded it as carefully as I could. We left.

"Mom. Mom. Are all those crutches fake? Did people really leave those behind because they were better?"

Louis' face crunched in an expression of confusion. I could hear his brain cells whirling with information he could not process. Martin shrugged his shoulders, picked up his penguin portrait as I gunned the car engine, one eye on the map.

"Of course it's real. You don't know everything just because you're two years older than me. Haven't you figured out yet that there are mysteries?" Martin sighed long and loud. I smiled, but the boys didn't see.

"Well, boys, to be honest, I don't know anything except that many people believe it's real. Sometimes believing in something makes something real, makes things happen. Martin is right about one thing. There are mysterious things that we don't understand. Maybe some day we will. So. It's still early. How about we drive to Los Alamos?"

The boys ate handfuls of our homemade trail-mix as we bypassed Santa Fe and hooked a left onto the isolated freeway toward Los Alamos. The road was lined with safety signs dictating an unusually low speed limit. Safety Corridor! Do Not Pass! 40 mph! We wound through three unoccupied lanes snaking through a heat-stroke landscape pock-marked with a million dinky wind caves, my foot hovering over the brake.

"Mom! Why do we have to go so slow? There's no one around."

Martin stuck his hand out the window and let it rise and fall with the turbulence surrounding us. Louis considered the question, and I watched him in the rearview mirror, his mind sifting through all the possible explanations.

"Well, the road isn't that steep. And it doesn't look like it gets a lot of traffic. Maybe they're doing road construction? But why's this road so big?"

He shook his head to himself. He knew he wasn't right. It didn't compute.

"Guys, I know the answer. This is the only road that takes you to Los Alamos. Here, look at the map."

I passed the folder paper to the boys. Two police cars huddled in the desert median, radar guns at attention. I continued to crawl through the hills.

"Los Alamos is where the Los Alamos National Laboratory is. Everyone in the entire town either is a scientist, a researcher, an engineer, or works for the lab or to help support those who work in the lab. This town is all about science. Nuclear science, for the most part. Sometimes they have to transport hazardous materials to and from the lab. The road has to be kept safe and slow for those trucks. You don't want a nuclear spill. I'm going to take the main exit. There's a science museum that tells all about the lab, so let's head there first."

The boys grinned. I heard the rustle of the map as they pinpointed our position, heard them whisper to each other about the space wonders they might see. I wondered, too, what to expect when we rolled into town. Our local paper liked to mention that Los Alamos held the greatest per-capita income in the entire state. Would the streets be green, lush, filled with sprinkler-soaked lawns? I rolled off the exit ramp, onto the streets of Los

Alamos. My boys hung their heads out the window like smell-starved hounds.

The town didn't notice us. It looked beat, tired, somehow poorer than my own cowboy town. Old cars lined the streets. I didn't see any Mercedes, any yuppie SUVs. Weeds poked through the sidewalks. The famous laboratory perched above the town like a high-tech falcon, claws gripping a mesa rife with juniper and rattlesnake, the only entries into its nest a series of gleaming security checkpoints. I pulled the car into a strip mall and cut the engine. The Bradbury Science Museum loomed before us.

"Ok! This is the official museum of the Los Alamos National Lab, gang! Let's see what the hoopla is all about! Time for some science!"

The sign on the door listed the rules: **No Food! Free Admission! Cameras OK!** The boys didn't stop to read. They tore through the entrance and bounded into the exhibit hall. Dr. Robert Oppenheimer and General Leslie Groves greeted me with stony silence. I stared at their cement faces, tried to understand what drives a man to consider atomic annihilation.

The museum surprised me, the way the town surprised me, the way it snuck mental weeds in its paved displays, the way it catalogued and supported defense, destruction, the cheerful stewardship of our nation's nuclear stockpile. My boys ran from poster to computer, from a replica of the Fat Man and Little Boy bombs to a six-minute loop film extolling the virtues of weapons testing. This wasn't what I wanted my boys to see. I wanted to see the forward gallop of new technological discoveries balanced by the karmic weight of our nuke-dropping past. I wanted reflection, a sense that we are tiny in this cosmos, that we make mistakes and strive to learn from them. I wanted the awe of new discovery placed in context with the blood money it took to arrive. I wanted to leave.

I didn't expect my boys to see the museum the way I saw it. I watched them press buttons and slide cards, imitate the motions of super secret scientists. I sat. The loop film started once more. The narrator began again, spoke in chipper voice about the Manhattan Project, explained that we dropped two bombs to end World War II. The camera cut from serious researchers to a mushroom cloud to waving American flags, a crowd of cheering, excited people. No mention of the deaths that followed, the way the land still carries shattered echo. I pulled a pen from my purse and drew a dove on the back of my business card. I set it on the empty seat to my left along with an Avon Super Shape sample. Two middle-aged men sat in front of me. They grunted approval when the loop ended. I noticed their laboratory badges.

"Mom. Let's get out of here."

Louis tapped my shoulder. Martin stood behind him.

"Mom. This place is all about death."

I grabbed their hands, and we ran for the car, left the heavy glass door to shutter behind us. I pointed the car home, back down the slow safety hill. We didn't speak for miles, not until the sunset-hue structures of Santa Fe filled the horizon.

"Mom."

Louis leaned close to the back of my head. I could feel his breath on my neck. He sounded on the verge of tears.

"Mom. We started at a place that's all about healing. And we ended at a place that's all about death. It seems like everybody believes too much. Those church people don't question things. They just believe it. And maybe those scientists who work on weapons don't question things outside of their science either. What's the difference? I don't want to end up believing in nothing."

I opened my mouth to speak, to tell him he's right, that science is a religion sometimes, that people get immersed in their world and forget it's a huge universe, but Martin beat me to it.

"Well if you ask me, they should marry each other. Then they would have kids that can think about both things. Because that's what's real. Both things. But right now all those people are lopsided. Isn't that right, Mom?"

"Yeah, Martin. That's exactly it."

Louis lay back in his seat. Santa Fe faded behind us with the sun. We pulled off the road at Pecos and watched a lone coyote hunt rabbit. She lifted her head to the twilight stars.

Neighbors

La ignorancia es atrevida.

Ignorance is courageous.

Little dancing girls on Bridge Street / Birdie Jaworski

Pennies

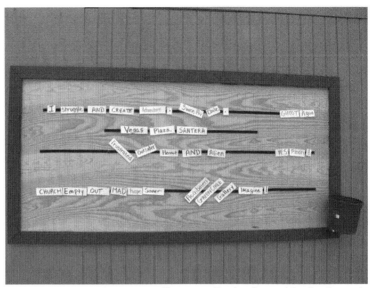

Poetry installation on Bridge Street / Birdie Jaworski

A young Navajo man sits outside the most popular breakfast place in town. Niyol sits cross-legged most mornings as I walk my boys to school, sits with the same ripped jeans, the same black sweatshirt that speaks of a thousand nights near the river. Sometimes I raid my penny jar and give him a small handful. My penny jar sits nearly empty, reflects the morning sun off its thick layer of coins, reminds me my days are spent collecting these bits of copper, a hundred makes a dollar, five thousand makes a good day selling Avon. He begs for his pennies. I beg for mine. No difference between us.

I passed Niyol the morning after first frost. I didn't have pennies to share. I gave my last change to the checkout clerk at Wal-Mart, the one with hands as skinny as death. She folded her arms and stared as I counted out six hundred thirty-five faces of Lincoln, handed them to her as I dropped five remaining cents in my back pocket.

"Why do I always get the ones with pennies?"

She spoke to the register as if I didn't exist. Time dropped her constant tug of invisible rope, and I stood a moment, a minute, all the linear vibrations of a century, my eyes dark and expressive, eyes of a homeless Navajo man, eyes of a thin-armed cashier, eyes on the consumer shuffle of those only slightly more content.

I saw Niyol as I crossed the street. I walked near the curb, left deliberate cowboy boot prints in the frost.

"Sorry, no pennies today, but here, have some Avon," I said, my hips near his head. I grabbed a few hand cream samples from my purse, let them float into his cup, and he reached out an arm and grabbed my moving leg just above my boot.

"Don't get lost!"

Niyol's voice cut the cold. I let him hold my leg. Sharp fingernails pressed through my tights. I felt them snag, rip. I towered over him, my leg frozen in place.

"I'm not lost. Not much, anyway. I hope you don't get lost, too."

His hand eased, and I shook my leg free. I reached back into my purse and grabbed all my samples, left them at his feet, some kind of guilt offering to a sweatshirt street buddha.

"Don't get lost!"

Niyol yelled as I passed the old pharmacy.

His name means Navajo wind, means change, means nothing because he's too poor. Selling Avon allows me to pass through a doorway carved far from comfort, allows me to erase concepts, projections, allows me to get lost, get lost.

I turned my head to see him once more as my feet turned the corner. He held an Avon sample up to his eyes, as if it were a holy monocle, an aperture to a land of pennies.

Extrasolar

My guitar class / Birdie Jaworski

I met a scientist. He stood in line at Wal-Mart, both arms balancing an overstuffed hand basket filled with Twinkies, Sara Lee pound cake, two Hungry Man dinners - Salisbury Steak and Chicken Cacciatore, a gallon of store-brand whole milk, a clear plastic box filled with butterless croissants. I looked at my own push basket. A dozen free-range eggs, six lemons, two bunches of cilantro, a pound of seeded grapes, a box of pressed soy, broccoli, a carton of organic lowfat milk.

"Heh. You must be one of those vegetarians."

He leered at my basket, as if it sprouted cantaloupe breasts. He held his goods close, but his girth prevented his nose from inhaling the imprinted cardboard housing his treats.

"I just try to eat low on the food chain. I have kids. I have to teach them how to eat."

The woman in front of me turned around, stared at my sparse goods, then moved her purse, her torso, so I couldn't measure her motherhood. Her toddler shifted in the grocery cart seat, tried to lurch and grab a candy bar. She screamed when her mom slapped her wrist, her yellow-ribboned ponytail cracking like thunder. I tried not to wince at my self-righteous words. I wished I'd kept quiet, just laughed at the man with the heart attack horn of plenty instead of handing him a shopping list of the ways I think I'm better.

"What the hell is a person like you doing here?"

The man laughed as he spoke. His groceries rose and fell with the shake of his belly. I knew what he meant, knew the Wal-Mart stocked tofu for the short list of people like me, people who came to this cattle-fed quadrant of New Mexico to escape the smog and traffic of California.

"I like it here. Where else should I live?"

He laughed. He liked my answer, and his cheeks echoed red like a school girl, as if somehow I told him those secret sexy thoughts I only dared uncork late at night when my boys slept under heavy blankets.

"I teach astronomy at the university. I wasn't planning on shopping, but I can't stop thinking about what's out there. I mean Out There. You know? Some of my colleagues think there may be as many as sixty-five Earth-like planets for every basic star we've found. If this ratio holds, we're talking sixty-seven billion habitable planets in our galaxy. One galaxy. One galaxy in a sea of countless."

I imagined it as his groceries jiggled. A tide of intelligence, as if every calorie in his basket was a planet, he was a sun, he was his own galaxy, a black hole at the center, a black hole munching Twinkies, gulping statistics, swallowing us whole, us whole.

"Huh. Sixty-seven billion?" I did a quick calculation. "At current population levels, that's about fifteen planets each for every man, woman and child living today."

The cashier started to ring my goods, my bunches of wilted cilantro carelessly shoved into a cheap plastic bag, my tofu, my hormone-free milk.

"Yeah," he answered. "Talk about vacation potential."

We laughed. I paid. I carried three bags and the knowledge we might be alone in the ways we understand life, but for all our smarts and commerce we're still insignificant. Just a few hours later I sat in a school room with four middle-school students. They rested guitars on their lap, just like me, and we played one chord after another in a rhythm that echoed a song they loved, a song riddled with illicit words, a song by a band called Limp Bizkit.

"Hey, Ms. Birdie!"

The tall eighth-grader with the kewpie doll hair and misleading angelic expression paused, three stiff fingers pressed into the neck of his instrument.

"Are you going to get in trouble for teaching us this song? Our other teacher makes us play baby songs, even though the stuff we like is just as easy."

I tried not to smile. I knew the other teacher, the man with unkempt hair who wore sensible brown sweaters over black jeans, who taught them old-school rock like the Beatles and The Doors. Kewpie Boy didn't know he passed them sure teen-aged terror, a cocktail of indecency and lust, songs that made his own teacher cringe decades ago. He didn't care what songs I brought to class.

The songs don't really change, I thought. It's all promise of sex, rage against authority. I wore safety pins along the bottom of my ripped shirts at his age. I shaved my hair into a mohawk, let my parents hate what I had become. I worshiped The Clash, The Sex Pistols. This is nothing new.

"Well, Henry, I'm going to tell you something I learned today."

He leaned close, as if my booming voice was meant just for him, not the entire room.

"There might be sixty-seven billion habitable planets in our galaxy alone. That's fifteen planets for every man, woman and child. I bet that any intelligent life on those planets has their own music, and I bet their teenagers think their music is the coolest and the best. It's nature, Henry. As you pass out of childhood you need to shake off all that uncertainty with music, with words you think might give you power. We all do it. Mr. John did it, too, and those songs he teachers you are just as wild. Listen beyond the melody, listen to those words."

Henry shook his head. He kept his fingers clamped into a C chord, and I could see the edges of his finger pads grow red from the pressure.

"Nah. I don't believe that shit."

He paused, waited to see if I would reprimand him, if I would react. I didn't move.

"No such thing as aliens. Even here in New Mexico. Heh."

The boy in the back rustled. He held his guitar on lap, too, but spent class pretending to play. He wore a mud-splattered black baseball cap over unruly black hair, black dirty shirt over frayed jeans - a loner, heavy with limbs that hated excise, heavy with some kind of invisible pain. He sat afraid, still, not yet knowing his hands could caress music from a hunk of wood and six strings.

"Henry, haven't you read Bradbury? Martian Chronicles?"

The boy kept his head down. I had to strain to hear him.

"Henry, we are the aliens."

I nodded, yeah, strummed the first line of our song, and as we slowly pounded through verse, through chorus, five students stomping feet, trying desperately to look detached, cool, my heart knew that lonely boy was right.

Muddy Example

My kachina, Mudhead / Birdie Jaworski

A Hopi kachina watches my computer screen from over my right shoulder. He wears a sanded leather loincloth over ochre skin, collar and cuffs of soft maple rabbit. He stands two-feet high, but he feels as tall as a man. His protruding eyes burn my back, transmit an ancient message of sure-footed joy.

You will dance and you will like it, he mutters. *You will run and you will jump.*

I try to pay him no mind.

"Hey, we're the same age, man. You can't tell me what to do."

Mudhead knows I'm right, knows we're both children of the sixties, his back rigid with curved cottonwood, my mind stiff with routine.

A rancher's wife handed him to me, made me take him in lieu of payment when I handed her a bag of frosted cosmetics and an invoice for eighteen bucks, thirty-one cents. I wanted to sell him on eBay, collect my fee by proxy, but Mudhead wouldn't have it.

You will keep me and you will like it.

He's a difficult Spirit.

The feathers in Mudhead's hands shook as I rustled the pages of my local paper in search of the County Fair schedule.

"Hey, boys! Who wants to help me bake a cake for the fair? I'm thinking I'll do a triple layer lemon supreme, whattaya say?"

My two sons barely removed nose from book. Louis, 12, raised one eyebrow.

"C'mon mom, you always win. Why not let someone else have a chance this year?"

Martin, 10, chimed in.

"Yeah. Besides, we don't get to eat the cake. Those judges are greedy."

I glanced at the two blue ribbons stuck to my wall with thumbtacks. San Miguel County Fair, First Place, Cake Competition, 2006. San Miguel County, First Place, Cake Competition, 2005. Maybe I have gotten complacent, I thought. I handed the paper to Louis.

"Okay, you guys think you're so smart. Find another category for me to enter."

I swear Mudhead giggled. The boys smooshed close on the couch, legs extended against my Spanish pine coffee table.

"Uh, mom? Will you actually enter the contest we choose?"

I shrugged my shoulders. Sure. Sewing, painting, pies, cookies, tortillas, I remembered the list, the old-fashioned pitting of gargantuan zucchini against watermelon, remembered last year's bevy of upstanding ranch women carrying tater-tot casseroles laced with green chile, carrying small town tradition in the crook of their arms.

"Sure. As long as it's something I can actually enter. We don't have a monster melon in the garden."

The boys whispered, laughed. They sounded gently sinister, the laugh of children giddy on newsprint power. Martin stood and handed me the paper, his index finger indicating my fate.

Mud Volleyball. Noon - 1 p.m. Open teams. Coed.

Damn that kachina.

The morning of the competition my boys brushed their rabbits. Martin checked Snowball's toenails, her tail, and packed her and Midnight into a cat carrier. The bunnies didn't care, didn't know they would be judged for size, weight, in the "Meat Pen" division.

"It's okay," Martin whispered. "The rest of those bunnies might get eaten, but you won't. We just have to tell the judge you're for dinner."

Midnight leaned one shoulder against the tight wire bars of the cage and rubbed.

My stomach flip-flopped as the car skidded into the dirt lot framing the fair. I wore shorts and a tank top, Walgreens sunglasses, my hair pulled back in a long ponytail. I never played volleyball of any type in the past, never cared much for organized sports, for the concept of a team, a group that must move as one. I stepped into the sun, into the tiny midway comprised of a few barns and several mobile units. I made the sign of the cross.

I like to do things by myself. I like to run, to move, to dance. I'm not that crazy about flying balls and muddy people. Hell, I'm forty-one years old. I'm not in the best of shape, either, not since the car accident last summer.

I tried to stop my mantra of pain, of worry, of Girl Who Can't Play Ball. My boys hustled their bunnies to the exhibition barn. I walked past the trailer serving up plates of greasy funnel cakes coated in icing sugar, walked to the wide ditch over which hung a drooping net like a useless apron. Several people stood beneath the net, waiting for any other takers, deliberately covered in mud like Dairy Queen chocolate dipped cones.

I chose a side, kicked off my sandals, and stepped into the mud. It oozed through my toes with a satisfying squish. It smelled bad, dead algae mixed with Lord knows what kind of field run-off, with the stale warm water from a rancher's steer-slobbered watering hole. A referee blew a whistle. He held a trophy, a statue as big, as bold as Mudhead, and I held my breath, dropped beneath the surface, let it coat my hair, my face, my arms-who-knew-no-volleyball. Rats. Forgot to take off my sunglasses first!

The game was on! I jumped! I ran! I danced, one foot stuck after another! I felt the spirit of Mudhead move my bones, move my bones, crack my back. I hit the ball once, just once during the whole damn game, and as I did, my boys screamed, "Mommmmmmmmmmm!" The muddy man to my left high-fived me, and as we slapped hands together, we both fell backward into the slippery muck. Score one more for the other team! We lost. Big time.

I let my boys hose me down next to the pig barn. A cute rancher in scuffed boots and a goatee grinned, shook his head.

"God, you were horrible. But I have to say, I never saw anyone have so much friggin' fun."

An Hour of Sunshine for a Million Years of Rain

Abandoned house next to mine / Birdie Jaworski

My New Mexican town forgot it once breathed, once promised railroad riches and mission salvation. I peddle Avon door-to-door in my usual utility kilt and T-shirt, scuffed boots against pavement. Back in California people weren't sure whether I was poor or eccentric. They didn't know I was both. Here my outfits don't breach protocol, don't broadcast silent messages. Everyone here is poor, is colorful, eccentric, so alive.

The house across my street houses six young cowboys. They rope lead-pipe steer in the street for practice, their lean bodies framing a block fence marred with teenaged graffiti. They don't care, don't notice the spray paint. I want to offer to cover it for them, dip brush into can and send a mural of horses and antelope and deep open sky across the cement, but I'm too poor to buy the colors.

I packed two bottles of Avon Wild Country cologne and two tubes of Wild Country Hair and Body Wash and a Mens' Catalogue in a crisp white bag and tossed in a handful of samples. I grabbed a few extra books and samples, too, and handed them to the cowboys in the road. They tipped baseball caps, waved me goodbye as I sauntered toward my new customer's home.

He lives two blocks away, in a decaying Victorian partly covered in cheap gray vinyl siding. I can see the pointed attic of his home from my bedroom window. His front yard looks like mine - lifeless, a camouflage yard of gold and brown deep in drought. I stood for a minute before I crossed the property, peered into my delivery bag to be sure it contained everything. He opened the door as I calculated and motioned me to join him on the porch. I stepped on pieces of chipped flagstone arranged in a crooked walk and met him at the stairs.

"Hey! I'm Birdie! Nice to meet ya!" I extended my hand in greeting, and he took it, shook it with strength and warmth.

The man looked much older than I expected, perhaps thirty-five, maybe forty but his voice sounded impossibly young, frozen. I remembered his initial call, the steady military tone of respect, the strange way he asked for products that would help him smell like a Marine.

"Hi. I'm Dante." He pulled a leather wallet from the back pocket of his jeans and opened it. "How much?"

I sputtered the amount and tried to think of a way to stall him, to get invited inside for a story or a snack. His hands were soft and delicate, not the hands of the local ranchers. He wore a faded navy blue polo shirt layered over a long-sleeved T-shirt. I took his money, thanked him, turned to leave, but I couldn't.

"Sorry!"

Dante looked at me with a quizzical expression. He reached one hand behind his head and scratched his coarse black hair.

"Yes?"

"Why? Dante, why? Why smell like a Marine?"

His lips turned up in smile, but my heart hurt a little to see it, a weary smile of some kind of aching regret. I cursed my big mouth.

"Nevermind, sorry! None of my beeswax!" I turned to run, wanted to jump over his house, over the two neighbors between us, fly home, sit on my stoop and watch the cowboys. But Dante cleared his throat, gave me an answer, something I didn't expect.

"It's OK. I should have expected you to wonder. I did ask you a strange question. I'm missing my father. He was a Marine. He died years ago, when I was a little kid. Died on duty. Some days I can barely remember what he looks like. I look at photographs but they don't make sense to me. It's like looking at someone else's relative. They don't look how I remember him. But I remember his smell, can't get it out of my head. I know he used Avon. Somehow that's all I have left of him. A few pictures. Knowing that he used Avon He smelled spicy. Like a father. Like a Marine. You know?"

I nodded my head. Dante nodded, too, took his Avon memory inside his home, closed the door. His song-like accent followed me home, made me wonder why I tease my customers, let them be teased when I tell their stories. I opened a Wild Country cologne sample as I sat on my front stairs. The cowboys whooped and hollered, their tiny Latina girlfriends cheering from the back of a pickup truck. I rubbed the sample on my arm and breathed the scent into my lungs.

The Unusual

Eso es harina de otro costal.

That is wheat from a different bag.

Old Harvey Girls Home on Railroad Avenue/ Birdie Jaworski

Beyond Polaris

Early morning sky over my home / Birdie Jaworski

"She's old, Birdie. Old." Hector's ponytail caught the wind as he scratched the perpetual eczema rimming his right eye. "It took two-and-a-half million years for her light to reach us tonight. She might have been sucked into a wandering black hole yesterday, but we wouldn't know for two-and-a-half million more years."

Hector whispered this under the ancient pitch of cloudless night. I looked at the sky, at that tiny speck of gas and fury, of 300 billion daisy-chained stars that threw an endless curve ball, missed Jupiter, asteroid and comet, Mars, sprayed photon against my cornea in some kind of long-winded hello.

I tell this to my middle school students as we lie on the floor, eyes tipped toward ceiling. Nicole doesn't notice the spray of calculated photon against acoustic tile. She nuzzles Peach, her hand caught in his unwashed hair. I pretend not to see.

"It's the Andromeda Galaxy, guys."

My computer hums, spits a reflected image of Hector's tiny speck into the air, her two arms spread from a central core in King Tut dance, her skirt twice the girth of our own milky gown.

"The light we see from her each evening is two-and-a-half million years old. We don't know if she still exists. This is ghost light, guys."

Peach laughs, the belly of his worn hoodie rises and falls in skeptical eighth grade angst, in lust. My other students stare at Andromeda. Their eyes. That's what gets me. Their eyes. They think they don't matter.

"Birdie." Hector whispered my name. It sounded like prayer, drawn into the soft clap of one syllable pressed against the sky. His windbreaker puffed out from the wind, bloating its embroidered zia into a yellow-handed black galaxy. Jaime stood behind him, twisting stalks of sweetgrass into braided bundles. The wind caught a crow's contoured feather, its colorless shaft mottled with black as slick as Jaime's oiled hair. It dipped low to the ground, caught another thermal, rose in harmony with Hector's campfire. My arm darted - swift, direct - but I couldn't catch it. I wondered who sent the message.

"Birdie. Look at that tiny speck. Look."

Another blast of ancient photon, another question mark tattooed against eyeball. Jaime passed me a match, passed me ten inches of sweetgrass wound with twine. I faced the great plains, back to the mountains, to the relentless spring wind. The match barely lit the bundle. A thin stream of fragrant smoke lifted from my left hand.

"We live in the only place where these things make sense," muttered Jaime.

I stared at him, at his face in profile. He looked angular, ancient, a half-Navajo pitbull sent to pasture. Hector laughed.

"Birdie, you know he's right." Hector's voice sounded distant, as if Andromeda cut the air between us with her fragile light. "We're all half something. I'm half-divorced right now. You're always on the periphery, half here, half in some other world. None of us quite belongs to this world.

But New Mexico seems half inside, half outside. We kind of walk the path between paths, you know?"

One of my students watches the dust swirl in front of the projector. Her mouth purses. She blows, blows wind and the scent of lunch toward the light. The dust scatters. The light remains still.

"Hey, Ms. Birdie. It can't be that old, can it? How can anything be that old. That's not what I learned from Father George." Crystal sighs, sending the memory of mild green chile enchiladas into the galaxy. "If it really is that old, then God made the universe a long, long time ago. Maybe that's why things are so fucked up. Maybe He forgot us. Or died."

No one laughs. No one answers. It's a tough question. I point a red laser beam at the ceiling, trace the curve of Andromeda's swollen belly in one languid sweep.

"Andromeda's name comes from Greek mythology. She was the daughter of King Cepheus and Queen Cassiopeia of Ethiopia," I lecture, my voice smooth, mellow. "Who knows where Ethiopia is?"

Robin yells out a response. He knows half-everything, knows it all half-assed, knows Ethiopia resides on the other side of the planet, but he places it between Israel and Pakistan, in the no-man's land between Hindu pandit and Muslim cleric. The class groans, know he's wrong, doesn't know enough to know why, where.

"Andromeda was chained to a rock by a cruel king and exposed to a violent sea monster as punishment for her mom's boast of beauty. A handsome adventurer named Perseus found her, found her and fell in love with her. He promised her father he would free Andromeda if she could become his wife."

I have them, I think. I have them captive, have them chained against my rock, have them forgetting Science is Hard, forgetting Father George, forgetting foster parent and second-hand clothes. I have them.

"The king agreed. Perseus used miraculous weapons! He was strong, sexy, and swift. He killed the monster and married Andromeda. And that," I continue, as Nicole forgets Peach, her eyes riveted to the ceiling, waiting,

waiting, "is how all things are. The biggest elements of space like solar systems, like galaxies, the biggest heroes, the biggest problems, all revolve around a centered attraction. The smallest elements of physics do, too. Remember the atom?"

Hector remembers the atom. He taught me about it as we star-bathed under Andromeda's delicate wink, taught me that photon holds electron in a lover's spell, that Great Spirit lives in the motions of the particles, not the objects themselves.

"Birdie, you always have your nose in the internet," Hector laughed. "But I will teach you a few things tonight you won't learn from your computer. Why are we here, Birdie? Why?"

I wasn't sure what question Hector asked. Why were we standing on Leyba Mesa at thirteen minutes past midnight? Or why do we exist at all? The wind stole the last of my sweetgrass smoke and I bent at the waist to place the charred remains on a flat rock.

"There's no moon tonight. It's new moon. That's why we're here. To call down the spirits."

I didn't call them flying saucers in deference to Hector's organic religion. The wind died for a moment. The lights of Albuquerque rose from an ancient seabed eighty miles away. Leyba sat square against the northern foot of the mesa; asleep, poor, a small collection of chipped-tooth trailers, junkyard pitbulls miserably chained to rusty spikes driven tight into the red clay ground. We stood above the village, our feet carefully skirting the edge.

The last day of Astronomy, I gave my students the gift of ritual. I handed out Hershey's Kisses, one per hungry teen, and asked them to remove the foil covers, to hold them steady in the sweaty palm of their hands.

"On the count of three, we'll make a secret wish and place the chocolate on our tongues. You have to let it melt in your mouth; you can't scarf it down. That's part of the magic. You can wish for anything - anything. And because we are all together, and because we just saw the wonders of the universe, that wish will come true."

I counted. We sucked those kisses invisible, snuck a piece of Andromeda into our hearts. No one said a word, but the room felt loud, chaotic. I
could see the wishes as if they were etched into the side of a tin can class
spaceship, broadcasting fear and longing to a distant nebula. Nick wished
to be more than half-a-reader. He wished to lasso letters, to write the way
the other students did. Mia wished for a real family, not a half-time foster
home. I wished for more than half of a career, wished to find my path, my
calling, my heart's desire. The wishes made me cry, and I wiped salt and
sad water from my face with the pink sleeve of my shirt.

Hector raised his good hand into the sky, the hand untouched by Vietnam.
I felt it pull my own index finger, pull Jamie's fist toward the faceless
moon, toward the mysteries that want to stay mysterious. I blinked twice,
once for the girl I am, once for the girl I still might be. I blinked a third
time to be sure my eyes didn't deceive me. Hector's voice cried across
Leyba valley, a wish echoed against the wind.

"Look."

I Come in Peace

Murphey's Drugs, Las Vegas, New Mexico / Birdie Jaworski

A man called my cell phone. I didn't catch the call, heard the ring as the shower pelted me with heat and hope. He left a short message, just a macho first name and telephone number. I stood in the bathroom, heat pouring from my hands, dialed his number.

"Hi! Is this Rocco? This is Birdie, the Avon Lady, returning your call!"

I sounded ridiculously alive, bright, as if I stood on the corner of Frantic and Spastic holding a dozen pink balloons. I applied the new Avon Super Shape Anti-Cellulite and Stretch Mark Cream to my belly with my left hand as I listened to his plea. I tried to remember how many days I had been using the product, tried to tell if it was doing any good at all. Not really, I thought.

"Oh good. Good, good, good, good, good. I need an Avon Lady. Next Friday night. Not tonight. Next Friday. For a party. How much do you charge?"

He spoke in tiny bites, his voice a breathy growl. I stopped moving. My hand stuck to my belly, a dab of unrubbed cream beneath it. I cleared my throat.

"Ahem. Uh, Rocco? I am really not sure what you're asking. I don't hire myself out for parties. But heck, I might, if you need me to do makeovers or something. Can you tell me a little more about your party?"

I closed my eyes and waited for what I knew would be an unsavory answer.

"It's, you know, one of those bachelor's parties. For my friend. He's getting married next Sunday. We don't need makeovers. We need a girl. You know. A girl. I looked in the phone book but there ain't nothing like that around here. Julio told me to call the Avon Lady. He said you were kinda old but still hot."

I glanced at the hand pressing stretch mark cream into the belly that looked exactly 40 years old to the mirror in front of me. I squinted my eyes, tried to see beyond my own expectations. *I guess I'm not that bad*, I thought.

"Rocco?"

I used my sultry telephone sex voice, waited for him to say Yeah.

"Yeah? Heh heh heh."

Rocco giggled, as if the anticipation of having an Avon Lady shed lotions at his party was the biggest secret fantasy of his life.

"Listen up, Rocco. This is important. Avon Ladies don't strip. We don't strip. Not even a little. We don't normally attend bachelor parties, either, but I would be happy to drop off a nice gift basket of products from our Men's Catalogue at the start of your party."

I said "gift basket" like it was a chapter in the Kama Sutra, like I promised sixteen unusual positions with massage oil and sandalwood incense. Rocco didn't peep. I heard him breathe, heard his brain cells whirl into activity. Should he say yes? I didn't give him time.

"Rocco, I'll be there right at the start of the party. I won't come in, mind you, I'll drop it at the door. But this gift basket will be the.... best. gift. basket. of your friend's life. Now. The charge will be one hundred bucks, even. Can I expect a check or cash?"

Rocco mumbled his answer, gave me the party address, and I hung up the phone.

I pedaled my bike to Wal-Mart the day of Rocco's party. I left it tethered to the dented mailbox standing sentry by the garden department and headed inside, past a canned pyramid of refried beans, past the little boys' clothes, past toilet bowl cleaner and push-up bras and boxes of Little Debbie treats, straight to the clearance corner. Sure enough, I found just what I needed - a huge green woven Easter basket for the princely sum of one buck. I pried the pale plastic duck off the handle as I waited in line and handed it to the middle-aged cashier with my handful of loose change. She didn't blink, just stuffed it in a wire bin filled with hangers and discarded merchandise as I waved goodbye. I hung the basket on the right side of my handle bars and headed home.

My two boys watched as I artfully crumpled pieces of pink tissue paper and layered it in the bottom of the basket. I added a spritz bottle of RPM, a Mesmerize Soap-on-a-Rope, a bottle of Avon Bug Guard, and three discontinued (and two-year-old but still smelly) Avon vanilla-scented candles.

"You're charging how much for this basket?"

My older boy wrinkled his nose. I looked at the goods. The handle of the basket was discolored where the duck used to perch, so I rubbed it, tried to soften the harsh edge, but the oils from my hand made it worse. "Nevermind how much. This is Avon Lady business, young man. Now you two clean your rooms and get ready for your club meeting."

My boys shuffled down the hall. I heard them shove toys under the beds, hide dirty clothes in the closet, heard them change from school duds to Star Trek uniform in anticipation of the Sci-Fi Club movie night. I stared in my own closet. What does an Avon Lady with a gift basket wear to a stag party? I sifted through my clothes, looked for something demure, chaste, something that screamed No Stripping! A knock at my bedroom door interrupted my thoughts, and I cracked the door to see my youngest son in his yellow Science Officer's shirt.

"Yeah? What do you need, honey? I'm trying to get dressed!"

"Mom! Can you wear your uniform, too?"

Why not? I grabbed my Star Trek Voyager Captain's uniform, the full-sized one-piece one with the velvet piping I made for Halloween, and decided it was the perfect foil for a handful of horny bachelors. I added my gold-toned communicator pin and a pair of serious black boots and corralled my unruly hair into a commanding French twist.

"Ok, crew! Front and center!"

My boys fell into line and we marched to the car, the boys with stacks of dog-eared comic books, me with my gift basket and the directions to Rocco's house. I dropped the boys off at the recreation center as twilight hit our hills. I left them with an official salute and pointed my car toward the railroad district, the poorest section of town. The vanilla candles gave off a chemical scent as I passed the train depot. I rolled down the windows, hiked the fan up to "high," tried to force the sickly sweet odor as far away as I could, but other smells invaded my senses, made me roll the windows closed. Rusty cans and glass liquor bottles sprinkled the sides of the road like heavy forgotten confetti, the signs of someone's pleasure turned environmental hazard. The splayed body of a dead dog hogged the middle of the street. The legs and arms formed a cross like a canine crucifix, and I swerved to avoid it. The sun continued falling behind the Rocky Mountains. I switched on my headlights just as I found Rocco's street.

I parked my car nearly a block away. It was obvious which home housed the party. The thump, thump, thump of cranking bass shook the air. I felt my internal organs vibrate in time to Latino rap. I wished I carried a real Star Trek phaser. I climbed the rotten stairs leading to Rocco's door and hovered at the top. The unmistakable bump and grind of cheesy porn music wafted through the door, mixed with the clink and pop of a thousand beer bottles and the rap baseline, an unholy symphony. I brushed the front of my uniform, arranged the gift basket neatly over my arm, and took a deep breath. I rang the bell, but I could tell it didn't work. I knocked.

A scuttle of foot motion fractured the noise. Someone switched off the movie, and a pair of clicking shoes stopped at the door. I felt a cold eye inspect me through the peephole. I smiled my best Starfleet greeting. I heard the hard catch of a breath, then a Spanish swear. I wasn't prepared for what came next.

"Oh, man! It's a Narc!"

The sure hiccup of a deadbolt slid into place, bulging the door slightly out of its frame. I could see shadows running this way and that through the crack, and heard hushed voices in anxious code behind the relentless Latino rap. The man at the door didn't budge. I could almost feel his breath through the pine. I rapped the knuckles of my left hand against the door and yelled.

"Hey! I'm just the Avon Lady! I'm no Narc! I have a gift basket for Rocco! Open up! Avon Calling!"

The man's eye loomed in the peephole.

"Avon? Why you have that uniform on?"

He coughed. I extended my right arm with the basket and tilted it so he could inspect the contents. Several more pairs of feet collected behind the door, followed by the muffled sounds of pushing and shoving, jockeying for ocular position.

"That's no Avon Lady."

"Lemme see!"

"Who wears shit like that? Feds?"

"Yeah, that's the Avon Lady. I see her around town. She's got a, whatchamacallit, you know, a Yoda costume on."

"She's the stripper?"

The deadbolt released and the door opened. Five young men stepped back, let me enter. Another half-dozen guys milled about in the background.

Empty pizza boxes covered every possible surface in the room, and the spaces between them were accented by empty Tecate cans. The room smelled like pepperoni and green chile and booze and pot. A poster of Che Guevara hung lopsided over a beige chenille couch. A pile of rented adult DVDs sat on the floor. I almost stepped on one sporting a bleach-blonde Latina's generous backside.

One of the crowd stepped forward. He wore low-slung baggy jeans and a black t-shirt with the Virgin of Guadalupe on the back.

"I'm Rocco."

He pulled a canvas wallet from a back pocket and removed some bills. We exchanged goods.

"So are you like the Avon Police? Heh heh."

The men laughed. I held the money in my hand. My uniform had no pockets.

"I'm a Starfleet Captain. Ever see Star Trek?"

The men shrugged their shoulders in unison. I couldn't tell if they meant Yes or No.

"Well, it's a little different than what you were watching before I arrived. Now, I don't know who the lucky guy is, but this gift basket has some items that will make you irresistible to your sweetie. I wish you a wonderful life!"

I turned to leave with a short wave.

"Hey, Lady! Wait!"

Rocco motioned to his posse to sit. They meandered to the couch, to the floor, pushing boxes, crusts, and cans out of the way, one of them parking his butt on a stained particleboard coffee table. Rocco handed the gift basket to a slight man in black canvas pants and a wife beater. He pawed through the contents, lifted the paper with the Bust Sculpt instructions to his eyes, held it close. His lips moved as he read.

"So why you wearing Star Wars? This some kind of joke?"

Rocco's voice challenged me, chastised me, accused me of interrupting their stag party with some kind of white chick slap in the face. I stood for a moment, my heart beating too fast, too scared. The rap song ended and a new song began, one I knew, an upbeat love ballad called "Es Por Ti" by sultry singing hunk, Juanes.

"Hey, I love this song!"

I paused, let the music move through my uniform, find my heart, let it slow, slow, make my pulse match its gentle beat. I closed my eyes, tried to think of a way out the door, a way out of trouble.

"Rocco, come here. Let's dance."

The men Wooooooo'd, fanned themselves in fake passion. Rocco's eyes grew wide. He didn't know what to do. I raised one Spock eyebrow and motioned to him with one finger and my lopsided smile.

"Come on, Rocco. I love this song."

Rocco grinned and moved forward. I lifted my collar away from my neck and stuffed my cash inside my bra. The men giggled. I aligned my body and arms to dance the Cumbia. I figured he would remember the steps from childhood, from a Grandmom or aunt with Latin culture on her mind. He took position, and we danced. He smelled like pot, like six bottles of aftershave, like chile and beer. He knew the steps and I let him lead me through the minefield of bachelor excess.

"Listen, Rocco. I wore this outfit because my son asked me to. Star Trek is cool. It gives my boys hope that our world isn't lost. You should watch it some time."

I whispered my message as the song ended. The men-boys clapped and nodded in satisfaction.

"She's all right. She can dance."

I waved goodbye, let myself out the door. One plaintive cry followed me outside.

"Hey! Ain't she gonna strip?"

This story would end here, with me a hundred bucks richer, one dance older, one stag party wiser, but something I didn't expect happened. I stood in line at the drug store last week, still recovering from strep throat, a bag of strong cherry lozenges in my hand. A man walked past me, a man I recognized. A man from the party. He hovered next to me, rubbed his mustache with his hand, then lifted it in the split-fingered Vulcan salute any Star Trek fan knows.

"Larga vida y prosperidad."

I Walk the Line

The Scientologist's Mesa / Birdie Jaworski

The Church of Scientology constructed an elaborate underground bunker to store the works of L. Ron Hubbard just twenty miles from my home. They cut it in secret, deep into steep sides of a scrub-tiled mesa in the middlest of middle nowhere. My son, Louis, 11, told me this as we drove through parched piñon-lined winter ranches in late December.

"Mom, listen, you gotta hear this!"

He rattled off a list of rumored facts - something about steel-lined tunnels, two UFO landing pads carved into sold rock, and titanium-etched records that can be played on a solar-powered turn table. I didn't hear his words. My throat gathered in a mother's lump at the new deepening of his voice, the way he held the newspaper folded in half with hands so much like a man's. He leaned forward and poked me in the side and my hands jumped, let the car lurch toward a nest of resting cattle.

"Mom! The bunker can survive a nuclear blast! The Scientologists say that after a blast the words of L. Ron Hubbard will be more important than ever."

Louis snickered at this last part. His dark cowlick fell over one eye, and I noticed again how he looked more like me than any of my other children. He continued reading the news article to himself while his younger brother, Martin, 8, cocked his head to the side to read an advertisement for a movie about an overgrown ape.

He has the unyielding skepticism of his father, I thought. *We know the future from the seeds we plant today. We can let our minds stray far into a black tomorrow, look at the trail of memory behind us, know what loaded weapons me might need to carry under our arms. Maybe the Scientologists need those books tucked into the furrows once dotted with Spanish missions, the space once inhabited by graceful people of the ancient lands. Maybe they just need to know they are safe, protected by nature's arid indifference.*

"Oh, Mom!" Louis raised head from the paper once more with an expression of surprise and haughty delight. "I'm taller than Tom Cruise! Hey, what's a thetan?"

I tried not to let him see me giggle. The road curved past the two radio towers signaling across the start of the Great Plains. I saw my tiny town below us, cradled by the New Mexican Rockies.

"You see the town?" I pointed in the general direction of our house, kept my voice level and simple, the tone of the mother trying to teach a lesson. "We live among ten thousand people. Some of them are taller than you. Some of them are shorter. Some are smarter, or more musical, or better at Chinese checkers. Now as for thetans, I have no earthly idea what the heck they are. Some kind of Scientology belief."

I searched "thetans" on the internet that night while 11 looked over my shoulder. According to Scientology, the thetan is the spiritual being. The thetan is the individual, another word for soul. We read a lot more about thetans, too, from websites critical and concerned. We read about the collection of expensive fees, about people who claimed cult, about people who claimed spiritual salvation. What a complicated, expensive mess.

"Come on, Mom. Can you sell Avon at the secret compound? Can I come?" Louis pushed my hands off the keyboard and clicked a link showing a topological map of the Scientologists' mystery archive. "Come on, Mom! Tom Cruise is rich! You read all that stuff about them making a lot of money with those classes. You might sell a lot of makeup."

The boy had a point. I printed out the map, and opened my word processing program to make a targeted flier for my potential new rich and unusual customers. **Lipsticks that every thetan needs! Ten tips for looking great at your next Audit! Beauty Secrets not found in Dianetics!** I folded my fliers in half and stuffed them into the latest Avon brochures along with samples for the new Avon Anew Age Intensive Treatment. Even thetans gotta worry about wrinkles, I figured.

"OK, kids! Let's hit the road! We need a good adventure! Louis, you're in charge of navigation and the binoculars. Let's see if we can locate the front door to this mystery mound. Martin, you're in charge of snack dispersal! I'll watch the Avon. Keep your eyes peeled for Tom and Katie!"

We piled into my car, faced East, headed down Highway 104 toward the forgotten village of Trujillo, toward the unknown, eating Fritos and drinking bottles of Carizozo cherry cider.

"Mom, do you think we'll find it? Do you think they'll buy some Avon?" Louis cleared his throat and picked up the glossy tabloid I purchased as we filled our tank with gas. "Why do people believe this stuff anyway? It says here that the Scientologists think an alien named Xenu stuffed us full of evil spirits. That's crazy."

He rested his head against the window, his eyes scanning left to right as he read about a pilot who flew over the secret compound. I knew he didn't expect an answer. I kept silent. I thought about the Avon samples I taped inside the brochures, tiny lipsticks in cherry and sandalwood, the new Anew Intensive Age Treatment for Day, rub-on fragrance swatches of Imari and Today. Do Scientologists wear makeup? Do they eschew matters of the flesh? I wasn't sure, only knew that this trip was for my boys, for me, a way to pass time in our new town, a means of gathering new dust on our feet.

We turned with the highway at Trujillo. A black dog with open sores lay at the entrance to a vacant service station, his tail wagged, hit the side of the old-fashioned pumps. A swarm of flies rose from his body, fell again.

"Mom! This town only has five houses!" Martin counted two mobile homes, a shack, a simple stucco residence, another, until they disappeared behind us, until we turned with the road again and the plains turned to red rock canyon, turned to a deep dip in the earth, and I slowed to ten miles per hour, kept the car from sliding too fast down the steep mountain.

Louis grabbed the map and matched our position with the satellite imagery. "Ok. Mom, we're almost here. Look, see that mesa?" I followed the line of his arm and pointed finger across the scarlet land to a huge oval protrusion of sage and rock and sunburnt clay.

Martin squirmed in the backseat. He watched me watching Louis and he raised his voice in surprise. "I know why they serve Red and Green chili everywhere in New Mexico!"

I turned off the road, onto a hard dirt trail, let the car idle in park as Louis continued his search and map. "Yeah? Why is that?"

"It's the land. It's all red and green. This is a Christmas canyon."

I stepped out of the car. Martin was right. The land spoke of chilies and twinkling lights, all the shades of ochre and sage an artist can create, all the shades beyond the palette. I raised my digital camera and began snapping pictures of the Scientologist's mesa, my body just yards away from the rise of ground, while 11 gazed at the top with his spy glasses and Martin ran free, collecting bits of rock and pebble to take home.

I wonder how long it would take to hike to the top? I stared at the mesa, calculated its steepness, its height. We could take our snacks and hike to the top, get a glimpse of those landing pads, maybe see an entrance.

I turned to return to the car and nearly dropped my camera in surprise. A long black Lincoln sat parked behind my vehicle. My boys didn't notice. Louis sat on a boulder, the map spread between his hands, a pencil between his teeth. Martin kneeled on the ground in front of a pile of stones, lifting one on top of the other. I stared at the Lincoln, tried to glimpse the occupants, but the dark windows reflected the falling sunlight. My heart began to race.

"Boys! Let's get back in the car and drive around to the other side of the mesa, OK?" I yelled. My words echoed off the Scientologist's hill. I turned to look at the Lincoln, and as my boys ran to the car, a woman in a navy blue suit opened the door and stepped out.

"Excuse me, Ma'am?"

I handed my camera to Louis as he jumped in the car. I stuck my hands inside my jeans and flapped my elbows in greeting.

"Hey there! Nice day, isn't it? Don't you just love Corazon Canyon?" I watched Louis remove the lens cap of the camera out of the corner of my eye, watched him focus on Martin, snap pictures of outstretched tongue and crossed eyes.

"Excuse, me," the woman repeated. "Why are you here? Why are you taking photographs of that formation?" She pointed one well-manicured index finger toward the mystery mesa. The sun reflected off her careful mauve polish, and I noticed she wore a diver's water-resistant watch.

"To tell you the truth, I'm looking for the Scientologists. I'm selling Avon and I figured they might enjoy having a local rep supply them with make-up and skin care items. It's thirty miles to town and the only stores in town are Walgreens and Wal-Mart. Avon has better products than you can get in town, so I thought I might pick up a few new customers. Do you know about the secret archive compound? It was on CNN and everything." I kicked my right cowboy boot against the other and grainy red dust sprayed against a hubcap.

"Is this the formation?" The woman's hair moved as one unit, and I tried not to stare.

"Yes, it sure is. I have the satellite maps and this is it. No doubt about it. The mesa is distinctive, and it sits at the base of this canyon. The airstrip should be directly behind that hill and the UFO landing pads in that direction." I pointed toward the east, and my face grew red in embarrassment as I realized my fingernails weren't painted. Grit and Frito salt and the slight red stain of cherries dotted my uneven cuticles. *Some Avon Lady I am*, I thought. Crap.

"I'm researching this location for a news expose. Don't you think these people are crazy?" She leaned into her vehicle and pulled out a fancy camera with a telescoping lens, a tripod, a stenographer's pad with illegible notation in angled script. "The article is going to focus on the ways they keep people from leaving the church. I'm just here to get some photographs. You should stay clear of them if you're smart. You think you're selling Avon, but if you sell it to them I guarantee it'll be your soul next. Look at Katie Holmes."

I laughed as she drove the feet of the camera stand into the arid soil, thought about Tom Cruise's fiancée, thought about the ways I caved into the lifestyle demands of men in my past.

"We all link with things we believe bring us closer to the source, don't you think? Sometimes we pay a heavy price, though, until we discover we already hold the truth in our hearts." I scratched the small of my back, saw Martin lean out of his window, open his mouth.

"Hey, Mom! Are you talking to a thetan?" The backseat exploded into giggles, and I rolled my eyes. Reporter Lady didn't care. She attached her equipment to the tripod and held a light meter in her left hand.

"I don't know what you're getting at, but the Scientologist's source is spelled C-A-S-H."

I placed an Avon brochure on her hood, waved goodbye, left her to measure and capture the bounce of the sun's rays, and pointed my car West, with the plan of circling the compound until I found a point of entry. We passed a metal road sign, bent over from a glancing blow from some pickup truck or the momentum of the eleven bullets that pierced it into a piece of silent cowboy art. The canyon was far behind us now, and only an occasional juniper and piñon broke the sun. The land spread in lumps, rises and dips in the sand, some places covered in mold-colored lichen, some places layered in gold and black sand underneath the constant wave of dry grass.

This desert doesn't care about Scientology, I thought. It felt like it was waiting for something, maybe a meteor to crash out of the skies or a bulldozer to drive through, turn it into something smart and complex current.

The road stretched out in front of us. It seemed to roll on forever, past one rock formation looking like all the others, then another, then a slice of sandstone, then an ancient juniper. We passed a coyote. She stood at the edge of the road as if waiting to cross. I could see rough skin under her coat, a crisscross of scars and wayward tufts of fur. She looked like she knew something interesting about us, and I turned my head to keep her in vision. We watched each other until she disappeared, a tiny dot like her fleas on the horizon. The sun framed her body, low in the sky, orange and swollen.

I turned past the West end of Trujillo, onto a dirt road that swirled into a spate of ghost structures next to a heavy modern metal gate. Ah, the Scientologist's gate. I pulled up close, let the engine idle. I couldn't get the image of the coyote out of my mind.

I am like that mangy coyote. I roam, I am restless. I carry the bite of fleas and the hope of a next meal.

The boys jumped out of the car, ran to the empty buildings, and I grabbed my Avon and approached the fence. It didn't answer my silent request for a sentinel. It lay locked and angry, so I did what any good Avon Lady would do. I hung the brochures from the handle and patted it for good luck. I waited for the boys to expend their energy, then we shoved off for home. One mile later, as the sun grew tired and close to the ground, Louis yelped.

"Oh my gosh! Mom! I think the lens cap fell out of the car at the ghost town where the gate was!"

I swung back to the gate, parked the car, found the cap resting in the red dust. But something else caught my eye, made my blood run a bit cold with anticipation and wonder. My brochures no longer graced the fence.

I blew across the lens cap, sending a micro-wave of dust toward the Scientologists' fence. I didn't alert the boys, didn't tell them my brochures evaporated like our sweat into the arid air. I leaned against the car, poured bottled water over the cap, swished it this way and that, dried it on my pink western shirt. Louis rolled down his window, threw out a crushed Frito, sunk back into the bench seat.

I glanced around the ghost town, tried to see a moving vehicle or a walking thetan, someone toting Avon goodies. Nothing. Nothing but the dead skulls of cholla cactus lying in random piles. The gentle blue flicker of a television set rolled Morse code across the prairie. That ranch house is too far away. I wondered if someone hid behind the widowed church, the empty pineboard homes. The wind laughed at me, sent scattering shadows of juniper and piñon along the old truck tracks marring the ground.

"Boys, let's get outta here!" I jumped in the car and slowly backed onto the county road. I drove at a snail's pace home, wanted to breathe the gold and purple sunset. I switched on the radio and the pathos of country western music filled the car, flew out the open windows to the layers of deep colored sandstone lining our road. A lone red hawk chased us, swooped high above the rocks, then fell just inches from the road. I watched him fly low to the ground, his talons extended toward invisible prey. He was missing at least two flight feathers and the remaining ones were ragged and broken. I thought I saw dry dust rise from the ground to meet him, but maybe it was our exhaust.

I know why the Scientologist's stole this mesa, I thought.

They know it captures shadows, shadows of dust and ruin and feather. They rise like a Phoenix. It's a place of reincarnation, rebirth.

A desert rat ran in front of my wheels, dodged death. I watched him freeze in the rear view mirror, then shake, run back from where he came.

I thought my story would end here, in a dinky ghost town bordering high strangeness. I thought I would tell you I never saw those brochures again, that I lost two dollars twenty cents in books and samples on a wild thetan chase. But I was wrong, four weeks wrong, one hundred thirty dollars wrong. My phone rang, just this past week, and I answered it though I didn't recognize the number.

"Hello, this is Birdie." I held the phone between my head and neck while my fingers typed out an email response to a friend.

"Yes. I know." The caller held her breath for a moment. I opened my mouth to speak, to ask what the heck she wanted, but she dove in, gave me a list of lotions and Avon bug spray fourteen items long. Her voice was cultured, sophisticated. She sounded Southern California. She sounded glamorous, urbane, so far from my New Mexican wilderness.

"Yes, ma'am! I can certainly get all of these products to you! Now, what's your address and telephone number, please?" I sat, poised, ready to strike, my ever-present open Avon brochure to my left.

"Sorry, I don't have a telephone. You can meet me at the Trementina Post Office, just please tell me when the goods will be ready."

I didn't know what to say. She must be a thetan! No glamour gals live in the prickly pear canyons. At least I didn't think any did. I pictured the "Post Office," a dirt driveway and a simple home that housed the boxes of ranchers and recluses on the other side of the Scientologists' mesa. I gave her a date. I gave her a time. I gave her a laugh, too, but she didn't respond.

"Mom?" Louis pointed to the phone. "You'd think that enlightened beings wouldn't need so much bug spray."

The boy had a point.

Marlon Brando, Pocahontas and Me

Ghost town at Trujillo / Birdie Jaworski

My mysterious customer ordered eleven bottles of Avon Bug Guard and three fancy Avon Anew skin-care items. I set the bags shotgun, and the contents rattled as I gunned the engine. My camera fell from the dashboard to the floor as I crossed the highway overpass and I cursed under my breath.

The Great Plains outside my town spread around decaying homes, old rotting cars and washing machines, past lean stray dogs and brown men in cowboy hats and torn jeans walking, walking, walking long pinto miles to the fields where they drive horses and cattle. I see no other cars on these roads most afternoons, just me and my Avon, gray jackrabbits spotted with fat ticks and skeletal tumbleweed floating past overgrown irrigation ditches. The ranch women are grateful for my delivery of bubble bath and perfume. They feed me biscochitos and tea made from gathered herbs, and we discuss town politics under the watchful eyes of the Virgin of Guadalupe. Sometimes the cost of my gas is higher than my sales commission.

The winter rains forgot to visit this year, and I thought about those ranch women sweeping wind-driven dust from their porches.

The Scientologists don't light prayer candles to the Virgin, I thought. *They can buy a pregnant cloud with their millions. They walk on the same mesa lands but they don't know years of uncertain hunger.*

I tried to wipe those thoughts from my mind. I don't know what stress the Scientologists choose in this life.

I wondered whether my customer was a Scientologist or a ranch woman with a hundred fifty dollars to spare on Avon. I wondered when the rains might come. I clicked on my CD player and Neil Young filled the car with his prairie warble.

The road bent before me, turned from gentle mound to razorback mountain at a grouping of three ranches. My camera banked with the car, hit the seat mount with a scary crunch. The road steadied and I glanced down to see if I could reach the camera with my right hand, pull it into my lap. I could see the blue canvas of its strap peeking out from under the passenger seat. I tried to grab it, my head touching the stick shift, but my index finger barely reached. I lifted my head, put my eyes on the road, on the simple state road, to see three running cows directly in my path!

I slammed the brakes, drove off the right side of the road, my car skidded and slid out of control with a screech of black rubber. I tried to correct my trajectory before I rolled down the steep embankment. I remember it in slow motion now, the way my heart froze, skipped one beat, then two, my left hand tight on the wheel, my right hand shifting down with force, six thousand pounds of moving cow scattering just one foot from my plowing car!

The cows rumbled parallel to the road, their hooves half hitting pavement, half kicking dirt, a cloud of fractal ochre dust in their wake. My car skidded to a stop. I felt the tires sink into soft earth. Random gravel ricocheted off the sidewalls as the wheels stopped spinning. I tried not to move. My hand was still wrapped around the stick shift, and I felt sharp spasms of pain as I loosened my grip. The car sat, tipped at a precarious angle due to the steep off-road incline. I worried my shifting weight would flip the car. The hiss of an Avon Bug Guard spray bottle filled the car with medicinal fumes. Neil Young continued singing, oblivious to my predicament.

And maybe Marlon Brando
Will be there by the fire
We'll sit and talk of Hollywood
And the good things there for hire
And the Astrodome
And the first tepee
Marlon Brando, Pocahontas and me

I'm not sure how long I sat, left hand still cradling the wheel, body rigid and afraid, waiting for gravity to shift from south to north. Neil moved from one song to the next. The CD clicked once, twice, started again. The Bug Guard stopped its hiss. I didn't think, didn't let synapse tell me what to do next, just sat, waited, a lost Avon soldier at perpetual attention. I felt drips of sweat bead along my neck but I didn't raise a hand to disperse them. My trapped car breathed with me. I felt her shudder, rail against the wind, felt her dip slightly toward death. I didn't hear the white pickup truck approach from behind, didn't see it until it stood parked along the street just ten feet ahead of me.

I squinted to read the bumper sticker plastered to the horse trailer it pulled.

A particle confined to a box can only have certain discrete energy levels.

A horse's nose peeked from between whitewashed slats. I tried to make sense of the sticker, the physics of it. A man walked toward me, a tall man in snug rancher's jeans and a worn black cowboy hat. Neil kept singing, I kept holding the wheel at attention as if pressing it toward the left would save me from sudden doom. I reached my right arm across my body and pressed the open window button. The man reached his hand to his hat as if to tip it, but dropped his arm as the edges of his mouth turned up in smile. He wore a blue denim shirt with the top two buttons undone, and I tried not to look at his chest hair. I caught a whiff of black licorice as he opened his mouth to speak.

"Ma'am, let me help you right yourself."

I couldn't loosen my grip on the wheel. I stared at the man's face, opened my mouth to speak but my vocal chords refused to vibrate. His hair hung over his left eye, followed the curve of his cheek, fell past his shoulders. He leaned forward and grabbed the door handle. The sun flashed off a silver bracelet. He looked to be my age, perhaps, maybe forty-five, with deep

crow's feet and hands that looked like they'd seen years of manual labor.
I leaned back against the sweating vinyl seat and closed my eyes. I could
barely feel my feet.

"Come on, step out. You won't tip. I promise."

The horse snorted twice. I let the man grab my upper arm as I swung my
legs out the door. I grabbed my water bottle with my right hand.

"The cows." I stood, braced for vehicular impact, but none came. "The
cows."

I couldn't see the Scientologists' canyon from here, just rolling hills of dry
yellow prickers and flora I didn't recognize, and the first grove of trees I
saw since I left town. I stared at the clump of naked trees, how they grew
too close together so that their nets of tiny branches wove together in a
swaying carpet. My car leaned toward a dead river ravine.

"The cows." I knew I sounded ridiculous. I wanted to say "Hi" or
"Thanks" but my tongue spat bovine wonder into the dust.

The man laughed. I looked into the distance. Only an occasional juniper
and piñon broke the sun. I could see the hoof prints in the road. I kept
drinking water, little sips, and the bottle dwindled to nothing.

"Stand back, ma'am. I'll get your buggy back on the road."

He spoke with the short staccato syllables of the local Spanish, each word
sounding like a gentle question. He bent to examine the wheels, first the
front, then the back. He left me standing quiet as he eased himself down
the incline, back in time to a place where water once ran. I closed my
eyes, found my breath and listened, waited for the air to move through
my lungs. A lone crow flew overhead. A sound of wheels against the road
loomed behind me, and I turned to see another white pickup truck rushing
toward me, past me, into the future. The man rose from the ravine, several
large rocks cradled close to his body.

"What does it mean?" I pointed to the horse trailer, to the sticker with the
strange sentence. He dropped the stones near the front wheels, bent over
to arrange them under the tires, and laughed. I stared at his right arm. The

muscles were strong, developed, with dark blue veins under his chestnut skin.

"Don't fence me in. That's what it means. Don't fence me in, ma'am."

He laughed again, and I watched his hat press against the front side panel of my car as he worked. He wore black plastic-rimmed sunglasses, the kind you buy at the drug store, and the side closest to me was missing the earpiece. They fit snug into a thin dent where his nose met his face.

"I used to work at Los Alamos."

He finished stuffing rock under wheel and stretched. I watched him across the car, tried to estimate his height - maybe six foot one, maybe six foot two. His body cast a lank shadow over the red ground, and I tried to think of something smart to say.

"So you worked on a ranch out there?"

I rubbed my hands on my jeans to erase the sweat. The crow returned, landed on a barbed wire fence beyond the ravine and cawed three times.

"No, ma'am. I was a physicist."

He removed his hat, set it on the hood of my car. His hair shone like black fire, and I noticed it traveled half-way down his back.

"I ride rodeo now. Electrons and horses. It's all the same. You ride until you sleep, then you ride again."

The man knelt in the sand. He stared at the small pile of rocks he'd created, lifted one with specks of green and black, held it toward the sun, set it down, lifted another. His bracelet caught the light, cast spark and shadow across his chest. I could see a lettered inscription along the band, but his motions were too quick, too sure for me to read. He stuffed a flat black rock under one front wheel, a rounded red stone under the other. I wiped my forehead with one hand. He removed his sunglasses and stuck them in his front shirt pocket.

The cries of a bird in the distance sailed across the grassland. He sounded like no bird I knew, a long drawn death rattle call. It echoed off the sides of the distant mesa, and I could tell from the vibration that the bird flew fast, flew fierce.

"Ok, Princess Leia, let me slide inside."

I self-consciously lifted one hand to feel the twisted hair beside my right ear, one-half of my cinnamon bun pairs, and I felt ridiculous, like an Avon wallflower geek. I stepped away from the car. I wondered if my lipstick smudged into my cheek. I glanced at my black t-shirt and saw a ring of sweat around the neckline. Gross. I felt his eyes follow my spastic motions.

"Princess, I'm going to buck your car into position. Spin it. Spin. Everything has spin. It's what makes you move at an angle to the direction of the field, jump a highway shoulder. All of nature follows the same rules."

I didn't answer. The man ducked into my car. The top of his head nearly touched the roof. He located the adjustments for the seat, then surveyed the controls. He turned the key and the echo of Neil Young and rumble exhaust filled the prairie. I waved my arms, ran to the front of the car, grabbed his hat. I shoved it on my head, and it fell to my ears, resting on my Star Wars buns. He smiled, gave me the thumbs up sign. A scrawny black Labrador with a notch in one ear crossed the road a hundred yards ahead. I breathed deep. The hat smelled like licorice and sage.

Spin. I tried to understand what he meant. Jumping isn't spinning, is it? My car leapt once, twice, three times, then four, pushed the retaining rocks into sand-covered space, leapt the hollow, leapt the highway, landed parallel and perfect the very second Neil Young finished his song, rested just two feet from the horse trailer. The man leaned his head out of the window. His hair covered one eye as he turned back to look at me.

"You don't say much for a Princess."

I waited for him to exit the car, but he didn't. The next song on the CD started to play, and I watched the man lean toward the shotgun seat, bend out of sight, then reappear in one short burst. I couldn't see his expression. His hair covered his face, made a soft blanket across his broad shoulders. His arms moved as if he were arranging something. My customer's Avon!

I ran to the car and stood by the driver's side door.

"So Princess Leia is an Avon Lady. Interesting. I figured you more of a scientist yourself."

My mouth hung open, a cavern of silence punctuated with short raspy breaths. My spilled bags now sat neatly on the passenger seat.

"You look like a scientist, you know. I mean your eyes. You move them like you're moving the objects in your sphere of vision this way and that to see how they tick. Like you're ordering the world around you. I don't believe you've ever had a small thought."

He smiled. He raised his right hand and swatted the bobblehead parrot on my dashboard.

"I just sell Avon."

My voice sounded tinny, small, insignificant. The black bird flew overhead once more, circled our caravan.

"No one 'just' does anything, Princess. Everything you do is because you had an idea, a creation. What you do is your offering to the world. Everything connects. The smallest particles in your hands reflect the movements of someone else's hands many miles away. There is no 'just' in life. Avon is the same as rodeo and they're both the same as physics. It's all cause then effect or effect then cause. How many things in the universe change because you brought someone a bag of bubblebath? You might be surprised.

"I used to think that physics could change the world - that we would discover all these amazing things about the nature of reality and what God really is, and we would be essentially omniscient. And then I discovered that it really was the same old book, different cover, and that we already had all the spiritual teachers and lessons and abilities that we needed, that physics was just a fun an interesting science you could delve into and discover small new things, and like any other discipline, all it can really change is your own world. You might as well do what you love."

I leaned forward and opened the car door. The man stepped into the sun.

I lifted his hat from my Star Wars 'do and extended it. He placed it on his head. His bracelet caught the light once more, and I saw the words etched along the rim closest to his hand.

Just to be is holy

I stared at it for a long time, as he lowered it to his body, stared at the edge of his shirt, the bracelet, my eyes resting on his hand.

"My Gramma used to say that."

My eyes traced a faded scar running along his unadorned ring finger. I wondered if he'd hurt himself roping steer or chasing quarks. Maybe the mystery hands on the other side of the world found themselves cut by knife or thorn bush. I wondered if the simple phrase meant the same to him as they did to my religious Gramma, if they meant Sit Still and Do No Harm, if they were a reminder that life seems harsh and unfair but is timeless and serene at its center. The man glanced at the bracelet as if to remind himself what it read.

"Well, Princess, my Gramma used to say that too. Old ladies got us beat in the wisdom department. Now, that makes around twenty-five words you've spoken to my two-hundred fifty. How's about you tell me why Princess Leia is driving a Saturn filled with Avon in the middle of no-where?"

The man leaned his butt against the hood of my car, resting on his hands. His shadow crept across the asphalt and touched my boots. I cleared my throat, tried to decide where to start. At my first trip to spy on the Scien-tologists? The part where my brochures disappeared? The mystery phone call? I wrinkled my forehead and closed my eyes.

"That's a lot of bug spray in those bags, Princess. Must be someone near water, and there isn't a whole lot of that around here."

He smiled, and the lines around his eyes deepened. The sun fell another notch in the sky.

"Well, I think I'm delivering those to a Scientologist lady, but she wouldn't tell me her name. All I know is I meet her at the Trementina Post

Office. She sounded rich and hoity-toity, like she came from La Jolla or Santa Barbara. I tried to spy on the secret compound first but couldn't get past the gate and I didn't want to hike in and get arrested because I had my boys with me."

I paused for a moment, remembered my manners.

"And thank you so much for helping me. I didn't know what to do! The cows ran me off the road."

I winced in embarrassment. Boy, did I sound stupid.

The man laughed long and hard. He stood straight, wiped his hands on his jeans, and extended one in greeting.

"Well, Princess Leia, visitor from a land far, far away, with a herd of angry dark force cows on your tail and a light saber pointed at the Scientologists, my name is Leo. Now, I'm no Jedi knight, Princess, but I know how to use the force, and if you're asking, I can find you a gentle horse and take you riding up the back side of the mesa. Can't stop a cowboy from herding cows, even if you are a big shot Scientologist. What do you say?"

Leo met my eyes, didn't waiver, as he waiting for my response. I hesitated, knew I was running late for my mystery Avon swap. I opened my mouth then closed it. I cleared my throat. I glanced at my watch.

"Princess, I'm not trying to kidnap you. If you want to see the Scientologist compound, this is really the only way." He smiled, ran his hand along the brim of his hat as if circling his head concentrated his intention, made it stronger, more able to withstand the wind whipping around us. The horse stomped one foot. Leo pointed to the trailer.

"Avon Princess, even Helena demands an answer!" The horse lifted her head in recognition. She seemed to agree with her owner, seemed to implore me to say Yes.

"I want to! I really do! I want to see the mesa. I can't right now, though. Not because of you! Because I'm already late." I cursed my throat, wished it would grant me better words, a smoother delivery, all the time in the world, a million dollars, anything, everything I wasn't and didn't have in that moment.

"So Princess is a responsible Avon Lady. That customer must really have a bug problem." Leo laughed, threw both hands in the air.

"Not really." I rolled my eyes and began ticking off a litany of my worst traits. "I can't remember anything, I get orders mixed up, I forget people, I give things away, if my customers don't have enough money I tell them it's OK. I've had a million things happen this past year. I can't keep track of the most basic things. I'm the world's worst Avon Lady. Seriously. But I'm trying so hard to be better this year! I promised myself I would get organized in 2006..." my voice trailed off. I felt old, defeated, too stuck in some kind of mind-time-rock-warp. I wanted to vaporize my customer, trail Leo up the mesa, take photos of strange celebrity money madness in the canyon. I wanted to pat the neck of a new horse, run my fingers through his mane. I wanted to hear stories about miniature particles and roping steer.

"Ok, Princess, here's what we're gonna do." Leo pulled a green canvas wallet from his back pocket and opened it. He pulled out a simple business card and handed it to me. His last name was long, elegant, the name of a conquistador from four hundred years past. Under his name swirled a lariat, a telephone number and three words: Cowboy for Hire.

"You're going to deliver your goodies, and you're going to drive home. You are not going to hit any cows. And when you get home, you will call the number on the card. We'll see the mesa when you have time. And wear your hair like that again. It's beautiful."

I left Leo with one of my Avon brochures and two skin care samples. He waved goodbye, his hair and his horse's mane both flowing with the wind, pointing the direction I should travel. I rounded the corner, wondered if I would take Leo's adventurous offer, dipped into the canyon, and skidded to a stop at the dirt road labeled "Post Office."

A young Latino boy with jet hair and ripped jeans wandered down the Post Office road. He carried a dish wrapped in foil under his left arm and a gallon jug of water in his right. He walked carefully, with small steps, and he kept looking at the dish under his arm, slightly adjusting it so that it remained perfectly level. A cloud of dust followed his feet, swirled in mysterious patterns that rose into the sunlight. He didn't match my wave, just kept walking, passed me, turned onto the highway and kept walking toward the Corazon Ranch.

I let my engine idle, tried to brush my teeth with my index finger and smoothed my Princess Leia buns down as best I could. I wasn't sure what kind of customer my strange maybe-Scientologist was, but she sure sounded cultured and beautiful on the phone. I glanced at my reflection in the rearview mirror and decided I looked a bit cow-worn but good enough for rural Avon. I shifted into first and headed for the Post Office.

I drove the dirt road like a jaded old lady, as if I'd seen it all already and didn't want to see it again. I mentally calculated how much money I would have to deduct for the Avon Bug Guard spray that was ruined in my off-road jaunt. With the diversion I was fifteen minutes late for my meeting, but I breathed deep, let the gritty air erase the cows, the cowboy, Neil Young, the despair I felt at life in general. I glanced at Leo's simple business card. What would it be like to wander the mesa on horseback? I tried to put the thought out of my mind.

There's only one road in to this Post Office, I thought. I can take my time, gather my wits. A jackrabbit sat on the sidelines, stared at me through one eye, furry antennas poised, ready for transmission.

The Post Office jumped into view as my car rounded a clump of scrawny juniper. It looked like a simple stucco home, a salmon-colored desert ranch home with small windows and a utilitarian sign with the town, zip code, and official Post Office title. I rolled to a stop, next to the only other car in the drive - a smooth black Lexus with tinted windows. Red clay clung to the wheel walls, and the exhaust sputtered as if the car had just been turned off. I stuck my head out my window and waved at the driver. She opened her door.

"Hi! I'm Birdie! I've got your Avon!" I grabbed the bags from the shotgun seat and jumped out of the car.

"Hi. Thanks for driving all the way out here. Hope it wasn't too much of an inconvenience."

The woman stepped out of the car, and I froze. Her hair gleamed copper and gold and artificial silk, artfully arranged in a messy updo fastened by an aqua and silver clip. But it wasn't her hair that I stared at, or her tight trendy jeans with the fashionable rips, or the off-the-shoulder teal peasant blouse that swayed with the rhythm of the mesa winds, or her diminutive height. It was her unique face, her wide-set eyes, the nose and mouth that I thought I might know from the movies, from the gossip-ridden web sites that chart celebrity nonsense. I wasn't sure. A flicker of silver flashed along the ridge of the mesa beyond us, and I jerked my head to see Leo riding his horse. He was only a wee bit bigger than a dot, but his hair enveloped his body like a Señor Godiva.

"Oh my gosh. It's you! At least I think it's you! Sorry. I don't mean to babble! Here you go. Um. The invoice is in the bag." My hands shook as I handed the Avon to Ms. Hollywood. She didn't crack a smile. Her lips remained rigid, swollen with perfection or collagen, I couldn't tell which. She turned sideways, set the Avon on the hood of her Lexus, and handed me an envelope containing cash. I wondered whether she was a size zero or two. Certainly no more. I sucked in my stomach, tried to look like a ten instead of a twelve. I tried to glance casually in Leo's direction, but I couldn't find him, his shadow, his hooved companion.

"I left you a little extra in the envelope. I hope you accept tips." She titled her head and the sun reflected off her carefully made-up skin. Her face didn't animate as she spoke, told me that she took cosmetic snake oil, believed in the power of eternal youth.

"Yes, I do. Thank you so much, you didn't have to go to that trouble." My voice stammered. I tried to gain composure, tried to recall the list of known celebrity Scientologists, but Ms. Hollywood wasn't on the list. I had to find out. She returned to her car, slid inside, and I ran to her window, leaving my Avon cash sitting against the windshield of my car.

"Excuse me! Excuse me! Are you a Scientologist?" I blurted the question as Ms. Hollywood gunned her engine. Ms. Hollywood didn't laugh, didn't answer, and as she drove away I saw the deranged expression of one clay-coated sorta Star Wars Avon Lady mirrored in the rear window of her Lexus. Rats. I waved to the mesa, to invisible Leo, waved goodbye to the Scientologists hiding behind the red and green.

I stuffed the money in my glove compartment and headed home. Why didn't I ask her why she bought so much bug repellent? I cursed myself for ignoring the obvious, for falling for celebrity, for the idea that one is better than another, one is prettier, more important, that I am somehow less. Who the hell was she, anyway? I flicked on my CD and let Neil Young sing about Pocahontas.

And maybe Marlon Brando
Will be there by the fire
We'll sit and talk of Hollywood
And the good things there for hire

When I got home I stuck Leo's card on the fridge. It sits there still, a memory, a gift, a reason to haunt the mesa sometime in the future.

State of Confusion

No Country for Old Men film set / Birdie Jaworski

When movie cameras focus on the dusty Mexican border replica spanning the University Avenue bridge, they will capture the dark hours before sunrise. A man bleeding from a bullet wound will carry a battered valise filled with two million dollars cash, money found in a West Texas field littered with a dozen dead victims of a drug deal gone bad. The man will hold his wounded arm and offer five hundred dollars to a passerby for his coat. He will stagger and fall. He will pick himself up, and with what little strength he can muster, he will hoist the valise over his head and toss it over the bridge, into the no-man's land between Mexico and sleepy border town United States.

I pictured this scene from Cormac McCarthy's disturbing novel, "*No Country For Old Men*," as I walked along Grand Avenue last week. The movie construction crew welded heavy steel supports to their convincing border station as the occasional vehicle exited Interstate 25 and crawled across the bridge into Las Vegas. I paused for a moment after I crossed the intersection. A scruffy man in oil-stained overalls reached into the bed of a pick-up truck and pulled out a piece of flat gray metal. He set it against the newly manufactured gateshack. A red Ford Escort with New Jersey plates gingerly crossed the bridge and turned North. The driver pulled alongside me and a woman in the passenger seat rolled down her window.

"Excuse me! You speak English?"

I turned around to make sure she was speaking to me. A man's thick Jersey accent cut across her shoulder.

"Of course she doesn't speak English! We crossed the frickin' border!"

I lowered my head and stared inside their car. The woman sported lethal red fingernails and curled hair sprayed to six times its natural size. Her breasts were barely contained by a gold lamé halter-top, and I worried as she unfolded a large Automobile Club map that one might escape. She turned to her companion and hit the map with the back of her hand.

"How can we be in Mexico? We just left Colorado two hours ago!"

My mouth hung open as they consulted the map. The man lit an unfiltered cigarette and flicked ashes into a styrofoam cup half-filled with old coffee. He shrugged his slim shoulders. He opened his mouth to speak but the woman smacked him in the arm.

"You be quiet! You got us into this!"

She turned to me.

"We're supposed to be going to Las Vegas. That's why we took the exit."

She spoke slowly, as if I might not understand. I laughed and pointed to the fake border station.

"Oh! You are in Las Vegas! There's a movie being filmed here, and that's just part of the set."

The couple stared at the bridge, at the signs welcoming them to Mexico. They turned and looked around them, toward the tree-lined streets pointing toward town.

"Movie set, huh? This is Vegas? Wow, that was quicker than I thought."

She grabbed the man's cigarette and took a long drag. She blew smoke into the air between us, and it hung for a moment like a murky cloud.

"So. Where's the frickin' Strip?"

Family

Cada uno lleva su cruz.

Everyone carries his cross.

Sissy (white dog) and Dante / Birdie Jaworski

All We Want

TUX VALLEY by Martin Jencka

My youngest son, Martin, turns 10 in a few days. He woke me an hour ago.

"I can't sleep."

He tossed his art supplies on the bed and crawled in after them. Graphite pencils, rubber eraser, ruler, a pad of heavy paper. I flicked the lamp switch, let the soft light compete with the moon's full glow. He lay on his stomach, eyes close to paper, and pressed the ruler against the page. One thin line, then another, parallel. A comics panel. I sat, fluffed pillows behind my back and reached for my laptop.

"Who are you writing about today?"

Martin looked at his empty story, as if my answer might provide inspiration. I flipped the computer top back and pressed the button that gives it life.

"Oh, I don't know. I have too many people to write about. I'll probably write about you."

The laptop gurgled, and I felt its warm footprint in my lap as it hustled awake. Martin stared at me, at my face in profile. His hair stuck out around his ears, and I thought about winter, how hair never hibernates the way our hearts do.

"Mom? Who writes about you?"

I opened my mouth to speak, then closed it. I almost told him about readers who liked my stories and said so on their blogs, about friends who mention me in passing, in short prayer. But that's not what he meant. He wanted to know who described my scowl on dry afternoons, who wondered why I love grapefruit more than any other citrus, who transferred my uneven skin tone to page, my penchant for singing off-key to every Lyle Lovett song, the way my hair snarls overnight, all my spoken, secret dreams.

Nobody does these things. I don't think anyone notices me these days, not enough to write when I'm not looking. That answer wasn't right, either, so I kept mouth clamped tight. Martin shifted his eyes to his paper. He began sketching a penguin, an action penguin with a knit ski cap, one wing raised in excitement.

"Hey. We both tell stories, right? I write them. You draw them."

Martin nodded. He added old-fashioned skis, a naked tree, a snow angel in the shape of a fat bird.

"It's our job to write about people. Some of the people I write about have no one to tell their story. But I have someone. Me! And you! We can write about people who need us, and we can write about each other."

He added another penguin to the page, a tall female with eyes almond and shrewd. My eyes. I smiled though my heart wanted to break.

"Mom, sometimes all we want is someone to write for us."

So here I sit, telling another story about Martin as he presses me into the page, gives me wings of charcoal, wings that sweep across three panels, lift me into heaven.

Chewbacca Rides Shotgun

Very Large Array / Birdie Jaworski

The clouds that blanket the Plains of San Augustin rarely notice the science traveler, the Mescalero Apache, the patchwork family with a bag of marshmallows and one unused match. The clouds push from Arizona toward Texas, push across the reservation, the dried lake flats, push past the twenty-seven radio antennas without a second glance. Every time I drive past the installation, I feel those wandering jewels mock me, tell me I don't belong in this wilderness.

Click, I tell them. *Click*. My camera speaks the only words we have in common.

I tried to describe the sky to Hector as he bagged my groceries. I wanted to tell him that his skin looked like the San Augustin clouds - mysterious, dark, rippled, old. I bit my tongue.

"Hector, I can't believe you've never visited the Very Large Array. It's incredible! Even if you don't like astronomy, it's worth the drive. The sky always looks like she wants to dump secrets, ya know?"

Hector shoved my jalapenos into the pink reusable bag I brought from home. He dumped a bag of rice on top of them, a dusty box of tofu, an ear of corn.

"Bye, Birdie. You need help outside?"

My Turkish friend, Ulak, grabbed the tote and grunted.

"No, thanks. We're walking. Good day."

I patted Hector on the shoulder and chased after my friend.

"Geeze, man. You didn't have to be so rude. What's wrong with letting him walk us outside? He likes to do it. He's my friend."

"Birdie. How can you let such an old man pack your food? He must be 80 years old. He should not be packaging groceries for young mothers. Where are his children?"

Ulak's long legs carried him across a vacant lot seeded with sweet grass, across Friedman Drive where the New Age acupuncturist presses needles into the taut skin of the pained. A starling squawked warning as we lifted angry foot onto compact dirt.

"Well, Ulak, he is old, but he likes to work. I don't think he has a family. Why not let him do what he likes to do? He's always so nice to me. Besides, I'm not a young mother. I have adult children now, and I am now officially middle-aged. Hector just wants to work. He probably needs the money. Heck, I know what that's like."

Ulak, didn't let his leather sneaker hover, didn't slow his long-legged pace. I struggled to match his stride, even though he carried the groceries, carried the heavy piece of twisted mesquite I found in the alley on our way to the store.

"You are not old. You are younger than me, and you look like a young mother. You are like that old man, you know. You don't let anyone take care of you. What is wrong with all you people in New Mexico? It must be something in the water. I think I need to visit more than once every six months. You need someone to watch over you. No camel route is long with good company. "

I stifled a giggle. Ulak let right foot lead, let his weight shift from one slim hip to another. His arms rippled with muscle, with years of hauling one bag of coffee beans after another. His salt-and-pepper hair flew behind him. So long, I thought. His hair got so long this year. We're all changing in ways we don't realize. He looks older, stronger, as if some artist continued carving him out of the mesquite he carries, carved a Turkish man on vacation in New Mexico, a man out of time, out of element, a man in love with an aging woman who can't love him back. I know I look my age, look forty, look forty-one, look as tired as the months behind me.

"Yeah, it's the water. Or the lack of water most years." I laughed. "But honestly, Ulak. Would you like me any other way?"

That night Ulak prepared coffee the way of his ancestors, let the ground beans boil with a thousand exotic spices. He poured sweetened milk into a tiny cup, topped it with the black pitch. My mesquite acquisition leaned against a stuffed bookcase, one end splayed with exposed root, the other pointed, firm, arching toward the sky.

"Birdie. Tomorrow we go to the Very Large Array. And then I must leave. You know I am returning to Turkey for a year to buy coffee and make new business arrangements. I wish you'd come with me. The boys would love it. My family is very wealthy and the schools are good. Please think about it."

I pictured myself in Turkey, in a land rolling more conservative, more modern, all in one breath, all in one confused breath, a woman with tattoos in a land she can't reveal them.

"Ulak, that's sweet, but you know I belong in New Mexico."

He didn't say another word until the turn at Socorro the next morning. The boys slept, still exhausted from a late night of Scrabble, from sneaking the rich coffee I saw Ulak hand them before bed. I kept my eyes on the road. Ulak cleared his throat.

"Birdie. Tell me again about the Plains of San Augustin."

He closed his eyes. The tires spun across a road tired of tourists, a road the Apache took when they left the reservation, a road covered in bird pitch and the skin of a thousand dead lizards. I let him rock to sleep. My cowboy hat pressed into my forehead, protected me against the rising sun. We passed the Bosque del Apache - a nature preserve filled with thousands of migrating cranes. An eagle squatted on a decaying cedar, his talons sharp and ready. He gave me the evil eye as my car sputtered past. I heard the flap of hungry cranes in the distance. Ulak snored. A strand of drool hung from the left side of his mouth. Ick.

I recited the story to myself as the men slept. The Plains of San Augustin. Llano de San Augustin. A flat place of deserted water, of mystery. A place said to contain the crashed Roswell spaceship. A place now studded with the Y-shaped formation of disks known as the National Radio Astronomy Observatory. Each disk measures twenty-five meters in diameter. I said this out loud, though I knew Ulak and my boys couldn't hear. But together, they create a virtual disk twenty-two miles across. We can meet the heavens here in New Mexico. We can carve the sky.

My charges awoke as I pulled into the empty visitor's parking lot. A sign warned us to turn off our cell phones, as our life signs interfered with Science, with ancient alien discovery. I pressed the Off button of my phone first, then Ulak's, as he groaned aware, stretched his legs below the dash. My watch read 9:00 a.m., still a wee bit too early for a tour, too soon to enter the Visitor Center and watch the endless film loop spout azimuth and incline.

We can watch the clouds and just rest as the sun continues to rise, I thought.

"Whoa."

My older son, Louis, age 12, scanned the horizon. The radio antennas stretched forever, one white flowering bud after another, each rising out of earth impossibly green with wild grass.

"Mom, it's not the desert anymore!"

Martin, age 10, opened his door. A blast of spring heat met our chests, our faces, our legs. The land shone green, looked strange, like a Midwest meadow, like the lake bed it once was. I glanced up at the sky, at the clouds moving in swirled formation, the beginning of a scheduled storm. I smiled.

Ulak stepped into the heat. His t-shirt clung to his back with sweat.

"Birdie."

He couldn't say another word. I knew this moment, had known it myself the year prior. You step into a land not-quite-New-Mexican yet all-too-familiar here, an intersection of wire and metal and sage. I lost myself in the moment, in Ulak's first breath of science-gone-loco. I didn't see the little black 'n white fella tiptoe around our car.

Spraaaaaaaaaaaaaaaay!

"Holy shit!"

Ulak swore! My boys whipped around - as surprised at Ulak's impropriety as they were with the stench that began to fill the field.

"Yuck!"

A skunk hustled toward the array, his tail high and mighty, tiny butt wiggling back and forth with aromatic pride.

"Fuck."

"Ulak!" My boys admonished him in unison. They laughed, too, as Ulak stood near the car, his body pulsing with disgust.

"Um. Did you bring a change of clothes?"

I sounded hopeful, helpful, as if my words would manifest a new t-shirt, jeans, sandals, and ten gallons of tomato juice to wash away the odor.

"Birdie. I did not."

I scanned the horizon for something, anything, to kill the smell. A garden hose rested next to the visitor's center, wound like a snake in the center of a small desert flower garden. What could a mom of boys do but the obvious?

"Ulak, take off your clothes. I won't take no for an answer!"

My friend spun around, tried to ascertain whether any other tourists might see his naked butt, and figuring he was safe, stripped down to navy boxer briefs and his socks. His copious black back hair stuck up in tufts along his spine.

"Ulak, I'm gonna turn on the hose. Sorry, this is one of those times where you're just gonna have to suck it up, okay?"

I twisted the spigot. Frigid water arched from the hose to Ulak's back. He flinched, screamed. The boys exploded in laughed. I continued to hose him down while offering instructions.

"Okay, now try to rub down the smelliest parts with your hands."

Ulak flipped me the bird. I squirted him in the butt.

"Excuse me? Hello?!"

A middle-aged man in khakis and an orange polo shirt strode toward us. His eyes still held sleep, still spoke of late night science, of listening to the pitch and roll of electrons against computer, of a wife most likely tired of abstracts and peer review. My boys leaned against each other, their sides against the car, holding stomachs ready to burst from an excess of mirth.

"Oh, sorry! We're just borrowing your hose!"

I continued to water Ulak. He held his hands in front of his boxers, but the cold water prevented any embarrassing displays.

"What the hell are you doing? What's with Chewbacca?"

The scientist nodded toward Ulak, who now was shivering from both the cold water and abject fear. I stared at my friend for a moment, realized that he did look a bit like a hairy visitor from another world.

"Oh, he got sprayed by a skunk. You know. Does that happen a lot around here?"

The scientist slowly backed away from us. He kept his hands ready, as if I the array had called me down from some lonely planet. I rolled my eyes and bent low to twist the spigot off.

"Ulak, you're gonna have to leave your clothes here. Your boxers, too. Can you imagine what they might smell like over four hours on the road home?!"

The scientist ran.

Two hours later, Ulak snored once more. My boys played rock, paper, scissors in the backseat, grand prize the last handful of Hot Cheetos. And my trusty cowboy hat - my beautiful black malevolent hat that knew the clouds of two hundred New Mexican afternoons - sat on Ulak's lap, shading his you-know-what from the desert sun. His natural covering of man-fur protected everything else...

Just a few days ago Ulak sent two postcards from Turkey. One for me, one for Hector. The one he sent me features a blue-tiled mosque glinting in the summer sun and a jaunty Wish You Were Here scrawl. Hector's is more simple - a man as sunburnt as roasted chile and a bored-looking camel in front of a sand expanse, not a cloud in the sky.

Hector, it says. *I was wrong about you. The skunk sprays the old and the middle-aged and the young. He sprays us all. May you enjoy all of Birdie's groceries.*

A Dance for Ben

Ben (left) and Martin in their finest! / Birdie Jaworski

My youngest son, Martin, 9, dragged my sewing machine across the living room floor. I heard it before I saw it, heard the bump and lurch of white metal scrape old oak.

"What are you doing! Hey! You're scratching up the floor!"

I ran from the kitchen, wheat flour covering my hands, my chest. I rounded the corner to see Martin bent at the waist, both arms extended. My Singer groaned as he pulled, a rolled comic book stuffed under one armpit. "Hey! Stop it! What are you doing!"

I wiped my hands on my jeans and a cloud of sifted meal floated to the floor. 9 let go of the machine, grabbed his comics, moved hands to butt and arched his back the way old men do when the morning cold hits swollen joints.

"You need to sew me something, Mom. It's an emergency."

A ridge of newly-exposed wood grain trailed behind the appliance. A thousand other nicks and pits eddied around the groove, a river memoir of running dogs and boot-scoot children. *What's another line in my life?*

Martin straightened up, thumbed through his book, flipped it open to page eighteen, pointed to a Star Trek Science Officer wearing a yellow jump-suit.

"I need you to make this. Today. Please? Pretty pretty pretty pretty pretty pretty please?"

I looked at the two-dimensional Trek Officer. His hair fell over his fore-head in tousled ringlets. I looked at Martin. His handmade red Command Officer's uniform still fit, still had room across the shoulders, an extra inch at the hem.

"What's the matter with that uniform? Isn't being Captain better than be-ing stuck pressing the ion torpedo button?"

Martin shook his head.

"Not for me, Mom. For Ben."

The sun dipped into the living room, bounced off of Martin's communica-tor pin. I lifted the sewing machine, my back still angry from a rough slide in early Spring's mud.

"Well, then. We better get to work."

I never found out Ben's real name. I knew it was exotic, Japanese. I met his mom during the school first PTA meeting of the academic year, when Martin was 8 and Ben was new, alone, afraid.

"My English not so good."

Youmei whispered when I held my hand across the table, asked her how Ben liked his new school. She wore loose jeans and an oversized sweater woven with rose blossoms.

"Ben only speak Japanese."

Ben sat at the end of the table. He wore the blue slacks the school demanded, wore his collared shirt carefully tucked, a vinyl buckle holding the ensemble in place. My son's hair stood in a kewpie swirl, his shirt stained, unrestrained, and I glanced with dismay at his untied shoes. He held his ever-present sketch pad, a well-ground pencil stub in his right hand.

"Hey, say hi to Ben. He looks lonely. Can you talk with him?"

My boy leaned across the table and opened his book to a fantastic spread of deep space. Two shuttles flew across a pock-marked moon, one gunning the other.

"Ben, do you know Star Trek?"

Ben grinned.

"Star Trek! Star Trek!"

Youmei nodded, barely lifted her head to meet my smile.

"Thank you. Thank you."

Youmei and I took tea every evening. She poured ice-blue solutions into thin test tubes in the local college chemistry lab. She didn't have a husband, a lover. I knew the topic embarrassed her. She came from a farming village in China. She attended university in Japan, met Ben's father, got married. Her face grew pink as she tried to explain the moments between Ben's birth and her arrival in my arid state.

"Men in Japan. They are different than American men. They see no wrong with take lovers."

I laughed, rolled my eyes, let the roll of my hand across the room tell Youmei my life was no different than hers.

"Men are men, Youmei. Men are men."

I took Ben under my wing, served him sliced apples and peanut butter crackers after school. Star Trek became our translator, our dictionary. My son drew pictures, spoke their names slowly, carefully as Ben imitated. I learned the Japanese word for "ship," for "Captain," for "best friends."

The boys acted out every episode. Ben was Spock, was Data, was all characters stoic, rational, full of science know-how. 9 was Kirk, was Picard, was the Captain with the muscles, the man who made brash decisions. I played supplemental roles - a conniving nurse, a slick reptilian creature, a human being made of light, my collection of dress scarves the strange vapor that could cause instant coma.

Youmei broke the sad news early in the new year.

"We have to move. Back to Japan. In the Spring."

Martin couldn't accept it.

"Mom, can't we let Ben stay here? This is the best place he's ever lived! He wants to stay with us! He's the first best friend I ever had."

I hugged him tight, pictured my nightfall cups of green tea, Youmei's fractured English and delicate manners.

"And Youmei is my best friend. Let's just enjoy what time we have, okay?"

The last Saturday Ben spent in our New Mexican wilderness Martin dragged my sewing machine across the floor. I called Youmei, tried to explain my plan, Martin's need to see Ben in the symbol of what they meant to each other. She didn't quite understand my mix of Japanese, Chinese, and English.

"Okay. Okay. I see. Okay."

Youmei nodded over the phone and I shrugged my shoulders. She would see tomorrow. Tomorrow. I sewed late into the night.

Youmei and Ben walked to my house. Martin stood sentry on the porch.

"They're coming! They're coming!"

He grabbed the freshly-finished Science Officer uniform and ran down the street. I placed the kettle on the stove, let the burning gas meet its bottom, added a spoonful of loose tea to my two best mugs.

"Mom! Mom! Look what Youmei brought for you! Look!"

I turned, bag of tea still in one hand, dropped it in surprise. Youmei held up the most beautiful kimono I have ever seen, held it to the florescent light with reverence, with love.

"For you. For you."

As the tea steeped, two boys ran through the brittle yard in Star Trek costumes, a branch a phaser set on "stun," and one woman from an Eastern land twisted a red belt as tight as she could around a crazy American.

"Best friends," I whispered, first in Japanese, then in English. "Best friends."

Six weeks later we exchanged photos. I sent one of me, my arms extended, as I twirled in my kimono under the naked New Mexican sun. Ben looked back at me, at Martin, his yellow uniform perfect, neat, clean, under a thunderstorm of cherry blossoms surrounding him.

"Mom."

Martin snuggled into my arms.

"Best friends are still best friends, even when they're far away."

Martin Cherryseed

Martin considers the comics / Berly Laycox

My youngest son crawls beneath my gramma's quilt these mountain sum-mer mornings. I brace myself to brave the scuffed pine floor in my bare feet as he flops on his stomach and places vintage comics on my extra pil-low. I leave him to my warm bed, leave him to carefully turn fragile pages, to become a penguin in a starched tuxedo, a lump-headed dinosaur chasing foolish researchers in some forgotten rainforest. His older brother doesn't join us, doesn't wake until I force his eyelids apart with a sharp shake.

Two days after school ended, Martin didn't carry comics to my morning bed. I tried to leave the sleep on my pillow, to drop it from my arms with a groan, a brush, but it clung to my skin, heavy, proud. I wrapped a chenille robe over faded men's pajamas and prepared to stretch my arms, my mind toward the ball of fire that hesitated along the horizon. My legs creaked as I formed the first asana. Martin giggled.

"Mom, you sound like an old lady."

His hands held a slim book with a worn cover. I didn't speak. My shoulders guided my extended hands to the floor. Hair fell across my eyes, nose, mouth, heart. I let myself become a triangle, downward dog, feet and palms flat against pine, butt in the air. Martin giggled again.

"Mom?"

He slapped the book shut.

"Yeah?"

I huffed my response. The sun didn't notice my discomfort. She stretched her rays across the Great Plains in heavenly asana, lent warmth first to the ghost town fourteen miles away, then the weed-caked airstrip where Lindbergh once landed, the criss-cross of arroyo and sage, the foundation of my home crafted from sturdy penitentiary tiles eight decades ago. I wondered whether those long-dead prisoners scratched notes in the New Mexican clay, left me pleas for cigarettes, for a perfumed letter. They paid their debt one small square rural home at a time.

"Mom, can we go for a walk?"

I lowered my butt, pressed my abdomen close to the ground, lifted my head. My hips creaked this time, a rich echo of ligament firecracker, and Martin imitated the sound with a raspberry explosion of forced air through pursed lips. I dropped the pose, let my chest rest against the floor.

"Yeah, sure. Let's go for a walk. The sun doesn't want my salutation today."

My son jumped off the bed and ran to the kitchen. I heard him open the fridge, heard the rustle of produce bag against drawer. He left his book on my pillow. "*Seedfolk*," by Paul Fleischman. I smiled, pulled a clean t-shirt over my head and remembered the story of a girl named Kim, a girl who planted dried lima beans in a garbage-filled vacant lot to try to make her dead father's spirit notice her, remembered the way the author let a new character speak each chapter, let them tell their own story of harsh life in the city, of the welcome sight and hope those struggling bean plants offered. Martin asked me to buy him the book after his teacher read it aloud in class. We read it at home together, then he read it again, once, twice. I heard the splash of running water, and slipped my feet into beat running shoes.

We headed out the door, into the alley, past the shack with the angry chained pit bull, past a graffiti-sprayed fence. Martin handed me a plastic baggie filled with cherries. I grinned, grabbed one, and sucked the sweet flesh off the pit. Martin ate one, too, but he didn't spit the seed into the alley like me. He stopped walking, bent low, and dug a tiny hole into the dirt road. He dropped the pit inside, then carefully covered it with a gentle pat. I shrugged my shoulders. We ate another cherry. Spit. Plant. The cycle repeated until we held the last two cherries in our hands. Spit. Plant. "Marty, I think it's great you're planting the seeds, but they probably won't grow in this alley. It takes a long time to grow a cherry tree."

Martin paused, his hands red with fruit stain. The sun continued her ascent, giving his fair hair a jolt of mountain fire. The parish priest hustled past us in his long cassock without returning our "Good Morning." The pit-bull lurched with a nasty growl.

"Mom. You read "*Seedfolk*." I'm just like Kim. I'm planting seeds where people say nothing will grow. And just watch, Mom. I will get to meet a hundred neighbors when my cherry trees grow, and they will plant their own trees. I'm making our town better one cherry seed at a time."

Five weeks later, those cherry seeds have taken precarious root. A dozen seedlings wink from the red clay. Martin and I surrounded each one with a little chicken wire barrier and a sign: "Cherry Tree Under Construction. Be careful!"

And yes, one neighbor, another, a dozen have stopped us, have asked about his trees, heard about his favorite book. I patted him on the head the other night and told him I was wrong, that one cherry seed can make a difference.

"Mom, there is no such thing as a bad seed."

Richer than the Sum of My Skirt

The old Armory building on Douglas Ave / Birdie Jaworski

My favorite skirt ripped last night as my son, Louis, 11, helped me take the clothes off the twisted rope hanging across my backyard. It caught on the rough tin edge of the garden shed as I swung it from line to basket, tore an uneven aqua letter L across the right butt cheek.

"Mom! That's your favorite skirt!"

Louis looked worried. He reached over, tried to pat the fraying L back into the fabric.

"What are you gonna do? Mom? Can you fix it? Can you buy a new one? You never buy new clothes."

I smiled, reached my arms to give him a hug. He smelled like the sun-baked clothes, like the ozone of our frequent monsoon afternoons, like new school pencils and little boy dirt. I realized with a start that he'd finally reached my height.

"Why would I want to buy a new skirt? I'd just look like everyone else! It's just a piece of fabric, honey. I can make a cool patch to go over the rip. Maybe you can help me design something fabulous!"

I stretched out the word *fabulous* like I was a flaming-gay television designing evangelist, ready to preach the gospel of style. Louis laughed, struck a fashion icon's vogue pose, and pursed his lips in elegant thought. The setting sun caught the highlights in his dark hair, made him seem even taller than a moment ago, made him shine retro, handsome, like some old 40's photograph and I tried to grab it, grab the sun, his hair, his height, his lopsided smile like mine, tried to frame it forever in some sturdy neural pathway.

Oh, please, please, please. Always be this boy, always be this connected to me, to the dirt on our shoes.

I pretended to take his picture with my hands held in front of my eyes in an angled square. I didn't want him to see the tear forming in the corner of my left eye. A yellow swallowtail butterfly glided by, landed on our basket of laundry for just a second. Just a second.

Everything goes so fast. I want to slow time, slow that butterfly, slow all of this, my backyard, the rising grass, the bunnies growing fat and sleek in their cozy hutch.

As the sky grew dark my sons both drew fanciful designs of starships and planetoids, the perfect foils for an exposed rump. I chose one design from each, hauled out my old Singer and covered the rip with a red picnic-check UFO. I added a long-tailed silver comet to the other side of the skirt, turned and sewed, slowly, slowly, watched the needle dragonfly down in the ritual my gramma taught me three decades ago. I hemmed two pairs of school pants, darned a couple of socks, tucked the boys into bed, and called it a night.

We walked to school this morning, walked the mile-and-a-half, me in my fabulous new galactic aqua skirt, my boys in freshly hemmed khakis. The morning wind lifted my skirt in the ways I liked, let a bit of this thigh show, then the other. My cowboy boots stomped on the sidewalk. I could feel the cool air rise through the bottom of my right foot where I'd stepped on a rail spike. Torn skirt, holy boot, pants to let out, beans and rice, walk instead of drive, hanging clothes in the sun, I chanted a silent litany of all the ways I desperately saved pennies. *So many years. So few pennies.* A blackbird squawked as we crossed a street lined with scraggly cedars. He dropped a feather in our path, and we hovered near the storm cistern as the feather twisted in an expanding spiral toward our heads.

I made the right decision. I've been a stay at home mom all these years, gave up a lifetime of career, a lifetime of adult interaction, years of slightly better comfort, better clothes, nice things to own. It's hard, but I know it's right. I barely pay these damn bills. But look what you have, just look. Look.

I watched my boys run ahead, run into the rising sun. Louis stopped short, turned quick as if he'd forgotten something important at home. I braced myself for a run west.

"Mom!"

He ran to me. His backpack slapped against his shoulders one beat behind his feet.

"Yeah? Forget something, honey?"

"Yes! I did!"

Louis held out his arms and tackled me in a bear hug.

"I forgot to tell you how cool your skirt looks."

Uncaged

Ramses eats GALLINAS Magazine / Asher Craw

At twelve years old, my son, Louis, stands nearly six-feet tall, but back in the third grade his need to understand shot to six feet, to the six books I would see him stuff in his backpack "just in case" the teacher assigned silent reading time. His classmates copied paragraphs from the Word Book encyclopedia for their science report on African Greys, describing the birds' natural habitat, but Louis dove deep, buried his brain in scientific paper and philosophical discourse. He typed a young naturalist's volume and accompanied it with a roll-out hand-painted poster of *The African Grey and His Family*, perched on some Congo tree, enigmatic, ready to swoop into the hot dry air.

Every trip to the Petco for dog food, Louis dragged me to the bird room to chat with a handsome grey fellow in a teeny corner cage. Fastened to the cage with a piece of dirty transparent tape was an index card with a hand-lettered warning in sharp, black Sharpie: *I bite!*

"Please please please please please please please Mooooooooooooooooooooooooooooooom can't we take him hooooooooooommmmeeee??????"

"Honey, look at the price tag. This bird costs one thousand, three hundred dollars. Plus, he bites," I'd sigh. "Someone will come along and give him a nice home."

But no one did. Month after month passed and the grey bird's price dropped to eight hundred dollars, then six, then four. My kid continued to harass me, citing examples of exemplary greys and their owners.

"Mom, African Grey parrots have the cognitive abilities of five-year-old child. They can learn to speak, in context, over two-thousand words. You can potty train them! King Louis the Fourteenth had an African Grey, and MY name is Louis. Besides, some scientists even think they're psychic."

The parrot would stare us down with one steel eye, with feathers rough and broken from constant caged boredom. We would stand at attention, our hands safely behind our backs, and intone the phrases man has uttered all these parrot-loving years.

Pretty bird. Pretty bird. Polly wanna cracker?

As we turned to leave the bird room the bird would catcall the wolf whistle, turn his lonely face to the cement-brick wall. It broke Louis' heart.

One night I ran to the pet store alone, but made my way to the bird room out of habit. The parrot perched in the far corner of his cage, preening his three remaining red tail feathers. The tattered index card was missing and the price tag was gone. I figured someone finally bought him and was preparing to take him home. At the checkout I made small talk with the clerk. "So hey! That African Grey finally found a home, eh?"

She scanned my twenty-five pounds of kibble. She spoke to the register as if I didn't exist.

"No, he has behavioral problems. The manager decided to euthanize him. They're going to put him in the freezer when we close up."

So the biting bird became a part of the family zoo that night. Louis named him Ramses, after the Egyptian pharaoh. I bought a huge cage on clearance and built a fake tree out of manzanita branches for him to perch on during the day.

"Ramses," I told him, as he shivered in fright and confusion, the new cage a silver monster in his five-year-old-child's mind, "I know you only bite people because you were stuck in a tiny cage for two years. I won't ever close your cage. Just take your time."

It took over a year of patience, of time, of allowing Ramses to bite me until he realized I would never, ever react with anything but love. Today he follows me around the house, chit-chatting, repeating his name over and over and imitating our nasal-voiced mailman. He's pathologically attached to me and tolerates the rest of the brood. Of course, Louis tells everyone he knows that he - personally and singularly - owns an African Grey.

This morning, I woke at four a.m. to write, to tell a story about my boys, about my New Mexican home so far, so different, from the African Congo. Ramses surprised me. He stood on my bed, feathers fluffed and preened. He finally uttered the words I've tried to teach him these past five years, the one phrase that until this morning eluded him.

I love you.

.

About the Author

Birdie Jaworski is the Co-Publisher and Co-Editor of
GALLINAS, a biweekly magazine celebrating the arts,
cultures, and communities of Northeastern New Mexico,
available in print and online at
www.gallinasmagazine.com

Birdie is the author of the Avon Lady Memoir,
"Don't Shoot! I'm Just the Avon Lady!"
which was nominated for a Pushcart Prize.

Birdie's life and stories have been profiled in the
New York Times, Time Magazine,
and the Wall Street Journal.
Her articles, blogs, and stories have appeared
in many national publications as well as
on National Public Radio.

You can read more of Birdie's stories at her personal site:
www.birdiejaworski.com

The author's writing shack in Las Vegas, New Mexico

Many of the stories in this book first appeared in:

mytinyvegas.com
GALLINAS Magazine
The Las Vegas Optic
The Las Vegas Times
and on
National Public Radio

Ramses says...

**What happens in Vegas
STAYS in Vegas**

4161358

Made in the USA
Charleston, SC
08 December 2009